The Silent and Soft Communion

The Silent and Soft Communion

THE SPIRITUAL NARRATIVES OF
SARAH PIERPONT EDWARDS AND SARAH PRINCE GILL

EDITED BY
SUE LANE MCCULLEY AND DOROTHY Z. BAKER

WITH AN INTRODUCTION BY
DOROTHY Z. BAKER

THE UNIVERSITY OF TENNESSEE PRESS / KNOXVILLE

Library of Congress Cataloging-in-Publication Data

The silent and soft communion : the spiritual narratives of Sarah Pierpont Edwards
and Sarah Prince Gill/edited by Sue Lane McCulley and Dorothy Z. Baker ; with an
introduction by Dorothy Z. Baker.—1st ed.
    p. cm.
Includes bibliographical references and index.

ISBN 1-57233-437-1 (alk. paper)

1. Christian women—Biography.
2. Women in Christianity.
3. Edwards, Sarah, 1710–1758—Diaries.
4. Gill, Sarah, 1728–1771—Diaries.
5. United States—Church history.
 I. McCulley, Sue Lane, 1946–
II. Baker, Dorothy Zayatz.

BR1713.S55 2005
277.3'07'0922—dc22   2005004398

Contents

Acknowledgments vii

Note to the Reader ix

Introduction xiii

"The Comforter is come!": The Spiritual Narrative of
 Sarah Pierpont Edwards 1

"My Chosen and only Sure Friend": The Spiritual Narrative
 of Sarah Prince Gill 17

Notes 93

Works Cited 107

Index 111

Illustrations

Sarah Pierpont Edwards, Portrait by John Badger   xxviii

Sarah Prince Gill, Portrait by John Singleton Copley   xxxvi

Acknowledgments

We are deeply indebted to many individuals and institutions in preparing this book. First, we would like to acknowledge Maria Gonzalez, Steven Mintz, James Pickering, and Roberta Weldon, who were the earliest readers of our work and who were kind in their encouragement and generous in their counsel. We are happy to thank Patricia Caldwell and Rodger Payne for their meticulous and rigorous commentary on the manuscript; our work is immeasurably improved by their efforts. We were very fortunate to work with two exceptional editors at the University of Tennessee Press, Joyce Harrison and Scot Danforth. At every stage they were both enthusiastic and exacting, and for this they have our appreciation and our confidence.

Keiko Cho Horton of the Interlibrary Loan Department of the University of Houston's M. D. Anderson Library was, as always, helpful in meeting our requests. The Charles P. Stevenson, Jr., Library at Bard College graciously provided us with a microfilm of Rebecca Ann Husman's transcription of Sarah Prince Gill's journal. This was Husman's 1983 senior project at Bard College, completed under the direction of Carol F. Karlsen. We appreciate the opportunity to compare our work with the earlier transcription.

We would like to thank the Boston Public Library/Rare Books Department for permission to publish Sarah Prince Gill's spiritual journal and for their enthusiasm for the project. The Portrait of Sarah Prince Gill by John Singleton Copley, a bequest of the Jesse Metcalf Fund, is reprinted with permission of the Museum of Art, Rhode Island School of Design. The photograph of Copley's painting is by Del Bogart. Joseph Badger's Portrait of Mrs. Jonathan (Sarah Pierpont) Edwards, a bequest of Eugene Phelps Edwards, is reprinted with permission of the Yale University Art Gallery.

Our final and greatest debt of gratitude is to Thomas Neil McCulley and Lawrence Baker for their unfailing support and the gift of their love.

Note to the Reader

The manuscript of Sarah Pierpont Edwards's spiritual autobiography is not extant, and access to this document is only through its publication in 1830 in Sereno Edwards Dwight's *The Life of President Edwards*. This edition reprints Sarah Edwards's text as it appears in Dwight, with two omissions: the quotation marks that open every paragraph to signal that the text was composed by Sarah Pierpont Edwards, and the phrase in the opening sentence, "observes Mrs. Edwards." The spelling and capitalization of the 1830 publication have been retained, including those elements that are currently considered unconventional or incorrect; these have not been identified as such with [sic].

The manuscript of Sarah Prince Gill's spiritual journal was given to the Boston Public Library by Edna C. Skinner of Tacoma, Washington, on August 1, 1947. The small book, 6.5 by 4 inches, is in good condition. According to Stuart Walker, curator of books at the Boston Public Library, the binding is sheepskin in the Cambridge, or paneled, style, making it without question of American manufacture. Walker describes the paper as handmade rag, laid, yellowed and brown, gelatinized, and hardened with alum. He noted that these characteristics authenticate the date of the manuscript as mid–eighteenth century.[1]

The text begins with a one-page undated entry that references the summer of 1755, and the second entry, dated Thursday, January 1, 1756, begins on the next page. The journal continues for 146 pages, with the final entry dated Sunday, June 17, 1764. Tucked between the last bound page and the back cover are ten loose pages that contain entries from 1743 to 1745. The fate of Gill's journal between 1745 and 1756 is unknown, but the entry of March 17, 1745, states that she continued to keep the journal "in other papers."

The 1743–45 portion of the journal presented the most difficulties in transcribing the document. First, because these leaves are not part of the bound journal, this portion is the most deteriorated, and it contains the largest number of blotted-out words and passages. Second, the signature "Miss Gill" after the beginning paragraph is puzzling. The author was Miss Prince at the date of these entries and was Mrs. Gill only many years hence.

This suggests that Sarah Prince Gill undertook revision of her journal much later in life. The initial entry is indeed retrospective and includes her rationale for writing the spiritual narrative. In addition, many of the entries from 1743 to 1745 exhibit fulsome reflection and narrative coherence that are not always a feature of the later entries. Gill may have endeavored to expand and polish her thoughts at the end of her life but did not have the opportunity to complete her revision for the later material. This hypothesis would also explain why the penmanship of the earliest entries differs markedly from the later material. Sarah Prince Gill's funeral sermon reveals that she was confined to her bed for the last eight months of her life. She perhaps began her revisions at this time in handwriting that was altered because of her illness, or she may have dictated these ten pages to a relative or friend. In either case, the voice and phrasing are Gill's. She must have valued her spiritual narrative above other material possessions to ensure that the apologia for it was committed to paper.

The aim of any transcription, of course, is to retain as much of the integrity of the document as possible while making it accessible to its readers. The following protocols worked toward that aim:

Gill dated nearly all her entries, sometimes even including the time of day. Her somewhat erratic abbreviations for names of days and months have been standardized to modern conventions, and her few omissions have been silently added. One curiosity that has not been reproduced herein is the frequent insertion of astrological symbols for the days, which were commonly found in almanacs of the time.

Gill uses dashes throughout the manuscript in ways that a modern writer might use a period, a comma, or a semicolon. The dashes have been retained in the transcription, except for the superfluous dashes at the ends of paragraphs within entries or at the ends of entries themselves. Though all modern rules of punctuation have not been applied rigorously, some marks have been silently added for clarity. Although rare, the abbreviation "yt" has been modernized to "that" and the abbreviation "ye" has been modernized to "the." Gill's spelling and capitalization, even the inconsistencies, have been retained. Readers should be aware that "least" sometimes should be construed as "lest."

Blotted out and illegible words are indicated by three periods in square brackets. Scratched out words, or pentimento, that are legible but are obvious "slips of the pen" are silently omitted. For example, in the second entry, marked "Eve," for July 18, 1755, part of a sentence reads:

"Under the Sermon in which a Glorious Christ was ~~described~~ displayed in his Personal & Mediational Excellencies—" The word "described" has been omitted in the transcription. This example also illustrates that the use of either word, while reflecting an authorial decision, does not substantially alter the meaning of the sentence. Some words have been added in square brackets for clarity and to complete the syntax of a sentence.

Introduction

In her seminal study of Puritan conversion narratives, Patricia Caldwell notes that this genre is the earliest form of public expression for lay citizens in the New World.[1] This statement assumes greater significance for early American women writers for whom the conversion narrative was the earliest form of public expression that was sanctioned and indeed welcomed. In fact Jonathan Edwards himself "requested" his wife to "draw up an exact statement" of her exceptional season of grace so that he could make use of her account to encourage other members of his congregation.[2] In this fashion he brought significant public visibility to his wife's writing. In the seventeenth and eighteenth centuries, women (as well as men) were encouraged to maintain spiritual journals, and at times they were required to make a detailed account of their religious life to petition for church membership. In these narratives the writer would record quickening or moribund spiritual affections, confront her objection to specific church doctrines, interrogate her attitudes and behaviors in daily life, and gauge her waxing or waning religious development—with the primary object of assessing the soul's path to God. Such documents afford the modern reader a singularly intimate portrait of the early American woman.

The spiritual narratives of Sarah Pierpont Edwards and Sarah Prince Gill illustrate in interesting ways the thematic and generic range of this form of writing in the eighteenth century. Some of the distinct features of each document can be attributed to its historical moment, with Edwards and Gill representing successive generations of eighteenth-century women. Other aspects of these texts can be understood in terms of each woman's marital and domestic situation. Edwards was a minister's wife in western Massachusetts who was occupied with the care of a large family and equally mindful of her public role in her husband's congregation. Gill's position as wife of a wealthy landowner in Boston and then Princeton, Massachusetts, led her at times to articulate a differing set of concerns within her spiritual narrative. Equally important is the rhetorical situation of each text, with Edwards's narrative ostensibly crafted for a public audience and with Gill's written as private meditation. Both Sarah Pierpont Edwards and Sarah Prince Gill were raised as minister's daughters and received the religious education and spiritual guidance that one would expect in this familial setting. Accordingly Edwards and Gill were well versed in the language and the themes of evangelical conversion narratives and other forms of spiritual narratives and, furthermore, were convinced of their importance. As such their documents evince their early training as well as their mature dedication to spiritual introspection and the social mission of their religious faith.

Sarah Pierpont Edwards (1710–1758) is currently known primarily through her husband, Jonathan Edwards, and his oft-quoted tribute to her, which he wrote in 1723, when he was a nineteen-year-old student and when Sarah herself was but thirteen:

> They say there is a young lady in [New Haven] who is beloved of that almighty Being, who made and rules the world, and that there are certain seasons in which this great Being, in some way or other invisible, comes to her and fills her mind with exceeding sweet delight, and that she hardly cares for anything, except to meditate on him—that she expects after a while to be received up where he is, to be raised out of the world and caught up into heaven; being assured that he loves her too well to let her remain at a distance from him always [3]

In this paean to the girl who would become his wife, Jonathan Edwards articulates in short compass the central qualities that he prized in a mature Christian life—perpetual contemplation of the divine, attention to God's order and rule, repeated awarenesses of God's gift of grace, an emotional and even sensual experience of God's presence, and fervid anticipation of the eternal bliss of the afterlife. That he identified Sarah Pierpont as a model of Christian womanhood suggests the important role that she would play in his personal life and in the continuing development of his theological thought.

Sarah Edwards's husband was one of the most renowned theologians in eighteenth-century New England, and many of his works—*Treatise on Religious Affections*, *Freedom of the Will*, and *The Nature of True Virtue*, especially—continue to be at the center of studies in American Protestantism. Modern literary scholars maintain the brilliance of such works as his "Personal Narrative," *Divine and Supernatural Light*, and "Images of Divine Things," while current historians and sociologists rely on his *Faithful*

Introduction

Narrative of the Surprising Works of God, and *Some Thoughts Concerning the Present Revival of Religion* as crucial texts for an understanding of revival movements in New England. Most of Edwards's writings were well known to the Reformed ministry in eighteenth-century America, and they challenged traditional approaches to religious thought especially as he recast Calvinism within the frameworks of Lockean psychology, Newtonian physics, and aesthetics.

An intellectual and a scholar, Jonathan Edwards was also an enormously popular figure and was regularly invited to preach throughout New England. In an age of many impressive and theatrical sermonizers, Edwards was not a gifted orator, but the power of his arguments and the fire of his language earned him countless admirers. More than any sermon of its time, "Sinners in the Hands of an Angry God" is recognized as the classic Calvinist sermon in theme and structure, and many of his sermons were printed many times over for the faithful in the eighteenth and nineteenth centuries. So too was *The Life of Brainerd,* his biography of David Brainerd, young missionary to the Native Americans, which was a bestseller in the colonies and in England.

Jonathan Edwards's theological positions and moral rigor attracted vigorous opponents, as well as staunch adherents, and Sarah Edwards supported her husband as he stood at the center of many social and religious controversies. Early in his career Jonathan Edwards took the position of "New Light" evangelical enthusiasts in direct opposition to New England's established "Old Light" ministry, and he then argued the theological principles and religious practices of "New Light" awakeners within his Northampton congregation. Edwards was convinced that a true apperception of divine things issued from the heart as well as reason. In this Edwards looks to passages from his Yale textbook, William Ames's *The Marrow of Theology,* which reads, "Faith is the resting of the heart on God," and "Faith . . . is an act of the whole man—which is by no means a mere act of the intellect."[4] Consequently, because women were recognized as being more emotional and more expressive of their emotions, Jonathan Edwards drew on the religious experience of women—his wife included—as models of God's engagement of the affections.[5]

Lest anyone consider his "religion of the heart" as a fully progressive or less stringent approach to Calvinism, Edwards also worked to reform the church's liberal practice on admission to church membership and to the sacraments. In this respect he was markedly more conservative than his distinguished and much-loved grandfather, Rev. Solomon Stoddard, the previous minister to his congregation. He worked to reinstitute the requirement of a personal narrative of Godliness prior to joining the church. Consistent with this position, Jonathan Edwards spoke out against the halfway covenant and instead reserved baptism for children of full professing members of the church. Not willing to risk profaning the Lord's Table, he also restricted the Eucharist within his church. Jonathan Edwards took his position as spiritual leader most seriously, and he exacted high standards of personal behavior for church members, asking especially the young people to forego many of the social pleasures to which they were accustomed. The success of his revival ministry and national and international prominence of his work notwithstanding, Jonathan Edwards was continually challenged to defend his positions within his congregation and within the larger Reformed ministry. In a conversation with his wife, he admitted, "It seems I am born to be a man of strife."[6]

Despite such controversy Jonathan Edwards was recognized and respected for his leadership in the evangelist ministry. At the end of his life, he was invited to become president of the College of New Jersey, which would later be known as Princeton University. This position acknowledged his intellectual achievements and continued scholarly vigor as well as his commitment to guiding the minds and character of young Christians, none of which could be questioned.

That Sarah Pierpont Edwards married a remarkable man is undeniable. Although her reputation in modern scholarship does not rival his, we can not assume that she stood primarily in his shadow throughout her life. A devout woman and an educated and energetic woman, Sarah was a full partner in Jonathan Edwards's home and in his ministry, a position that was recognized and valued in the eighteenth century and one that is becoming apparent to current scholars.[7]

The daughter of Rev. James and Mary Hooker Pierpont of New Haven, Sarah was born into a distinguished family. On her mother's side Sarah's great-grandfather Rev. Thomas Hooker in 1636 established the first church in present-day Hartford and is considered the founder of Connecticut. Another great-grandfather was Thomas Willet, the first mayor of New York City. James Pierpont, her father, was minister of the New Haven church for thirty years and a leader in the establishment of Yale College. Descending from noted New England ministers on both sides of her family, the devout, intelligent, and charming Sarah Pierpont was a fine match for Jonathan Edwards, who courted her while he was a divinity student at Yale. The couple married on July 28, 1727, when Sarah was seventeen years old, and moved from New Haven to the small rural town of Northampton, Massachusetts, where her new husband was minister. Jonathan Edwards served under his grandfather Solomon Stoddard, who was senior minister, and in 1729 succeeded him in the pulpit.

The life of the minister's wife was a public position with both social and spiritual responsibilities. Yet at this time Sarah Pierpont Edwards was also a young mother. Her first child, a daughter named Sarah, arrived in August 1728. Ten siblings would succeed the first-born girl, with a total of eight girls and three boys born within twenty-two years. That all eleven children survived infancy was an exceptional occurrence in eighteenth-century America. Even more exceptional, all of the children lived to adulthood. As might be anticipated, three of the daughters married ministers, and the son who was named for his father was called to the ministry.

The responsibility of caring for her large family was great indeed. According to Rev. Samuel Hopkins, a close friend of the Edwards family, the domestic chores fell largely to Sarah. He writes that Sarah "took almost the whole care of the temporal affairs of the family, without doors and within," allowing her husband ample time to study, pray, and write.[8] In addition to nurturing their children's physical development, Sarah and Jonathan were dedicated to fostering the spiritual growth of their offspring. Jonathan's concern for each child's religious awakening is documented in his correspondence with them, while Sarah's is highlighted in the words of their many visitors. Hopkins is effusive in his praise of Sarah Edwards as a Christian woman, wife, and mother.[9] Likewise the celebrated Rev. George Whitefield, who twice visited the Edwards home, testifies to the pious diligence of the young mother by pronouncing the children "examples of Christian simplicity."[10] Whitefield's compliment points to another of Sarah's many roles. That is, Sarah was not only a Christian mother; she served as the "example" of Christian motherhood for her husband's congregation. As a minister's wife she would live with a dual focus: attention to her private, domestic responsibilities and awareness of the public gaze on both her public and private actions.

Rev. and Mrs. Jonathan Edwards served the Northampton congregation for twenty-five years, during which time they saw a welcome increase in their church fellowship. In 1737, in particular, they witnessed an exceptional spiritual outpouring in Northampton and throughout the Connecticut Valley. Jonathan Edwards documented this religious phenomenon in *A Faithful Narrative of the Surprising Work of God in the Conversion of Many Hundred Souls In Northampton*, a book that is credited with motivating the series of fundamentalist revivals in New England that have been termed the Great Awakening.[11] With the publication of this work, Jonathan Edwards garnered national and international fame as a revivalist; thus, in great demand as a speaker, he was regularly absent from home while preaching to congregations throughout New England. During the early 1740s, in particular, Sarah Edwards was often alone in caring for her large family, hosting ministerial guests and visiting theological students, and performing the many requisite duties of the minister's wife within her husband's congregation.

Again, in her role as the minister's wife, Sarah Edwards served as a model of spiritual quickening for her husband, for her congregation, and for the larger New England Calvinist community. At the height of the Great Awakening, Jonathan Edwards documented his wife's extraordinary religious experience of 1742, a series of events that she also recounted in her own words at the time of her remarkable regeneration. Sarah had experienced a rebirth in Christ when she was six years old and was admitted to church membership as a visible saint when she was thirteen, after which, according to her husband, she underwent "wonderful seasons" of religious revival in 1735, 1739, and 1740, each of which signaled a maturation of her relationship with her God. However, Sarah Edwards's religious experience of 1742 was particularly notable for many reasons. Her spiritual awakening occurred largely while her husband was away from home, preaching to the congregation in Leicester, Massachusetts, while visiting ministers tended to his church. One could consider this to be a public manifestation of those spiritual attributes that Jonathan Edwards saw initially in the young Sarah and recorded in his early tribute to her. Her mind was "fill[ed] with exceeding sweet delight" and she fully expected "to be raised out of the world and caught up into heaven."[12] Her experience was not only an intellectual apperception of God's glory or righteousness; it was also affective and at times physical. She found herself unable to stand, and at times she fainted in her religious enthusiasm. The emotional and physical drama of this experience was deeply impressive to her and to members of her husband's congregation, so much so that, according to Sarah, one of the church members was concerned that Sarah was dying.

Within months Jonathan Edwards published his account of his wife's "remarkable season of grace," and he included it in his tract titled *Some Thoughts Concerning the Present Revival of Religion in New England*, although he never divulged her identity and even concealed the gender of the individual in his text.[13] While Sarah also authored an independent journal of her experience, it was published only in the work of her grandson, almost ninety years later. Sereno Edwards Dwight's *The Life of President Edwards* appeared in 1830.[14]

Eight years after the 1742 revival, Jonathan Edwards was dismissed from his Northampton church for a variety of reasons that were professional and personal, theological and social. Primary among them was the minister's orthodoxy. The congregation was outraged by Jonathan Edwards's commitment to restrict church membership to only those who offered a "credible" and heartfelt account of their regeneration in Christ.[15] In addition, although Solomon Stoddard had regularly baptized the children of members under the halfway covenant, Jonathan Edwards broke with his grandfather's ministry and refused to baptize children of individuals who themselves had received this sacrament under the halfway covenant but had subsequently failed to become full members of the church.[16] Similarly the congregation resented virulent and persistent claims that sinners who take communion are akin to Christ's murderers.[17] Edwards's sermonic rhetoric had frequently turned to divisive metaphors and arguments, pitting the "friends of Christ" against the "enemies of Christ," where the friends are those who subscribe to Edwards's doctrine.[18] Israel Williams, Edwards's cousin, probably spoke for many when he publicly accused Jonathan Edwards of being a "tyrant."[19]

The minister also suffered from his zealous and dogmatic posture in what became known as the scandal of the "Young Folks' Bible." Edwards initiated a thorough, public investigation of the young boys who poured over a midwife's handbook, then harassed young women with the sexual information gleaned from the book. The minister was disappointed that the young people whose souls he nurtured would be party to such lewd behavior and was angry when one boy defended his misdeeds and profaned the scriptures by calling the midwife's book "the Young Folks' Bible." In response Edwards launched personal inquiries, convened meetings, and spoke from the pulpit about the wrongdoing and, in the process, upset and embarrassed much of his congregation.

Additionally the community's alienation of the minister can also be attributed to financial concerns. While it is true that Jonathan Edwards regularly attempted to renegotiate his salary and that the congregation's committee never satisfied his full request, this was a dull and vexing aspect of almost every Calvinist minister's life. However, for the Edwards family, the issue of salary became personal and offensive because, as Jonathan Edwards put it, there were many jealousies expressed of me and my family, as though we were lavish of what we received and of a craving disposition and abused the town's freeness in their allowances they had made. And I perceived that much fault was found by some persons with our manner of spending, with the clothes that we wore and the like, from which, together with some mistakes of matters of fact, there manifestly appeared a considerable degree of disgust in many.[20]

As the minister's wife and procurer for the home, Sarah Edwards was especially sensitive to these charges, and on one occasion she wrote independently to the church committee asking for reimbursement of family expenses.[21]

Two years after the ministerial council voted to remove Jonathan Edwards from his pulpit, Jonathan and Sarah moved their family to Stockbridge, on the westernmost frontier of Massachusetts, where he worked among the Mohican and Mohawk Indians and wrote many of his major treatises. Sarah's life continued to center on her role as minister's wife, so she too devoted herself to the Native American congregation, which, according to her husband, was especially pleased with her attentions. At the same time, colonial townships in this area were constantly in fear of attack by the Native Americans. Daughter Esther wrote in 1755 that she was uneasy about a forthcoming visit to her parents' home: "I am not so sertain about going to Stockbridge for the Indians have made their appearance near Stockbridge, and I don't like to be killed by the *barbarian* retches."[22] Nonetheless the Edwards family found normalcy in its routine, which meant regular prayer, schooling for the children, religious study for all, singing school, outdoor sports, and correspondence with the married daughters who lived at a distance. Mary Edwards Dwight had remained in Northampton with her husband, Timothy, and Esther Edwards Burr moved to Newark with her husband, Reverend Aaron Burr, who was tapped to be president of the College of New Jersey in Princeton. Daughter Lucy regularly visited at the homes of her sisters Mary and Esther, and Sarah Edwards was regularly involved with her oldest daughter and namesake, Sarah Edwards Porter, who had moved to Stockbridge with her husband. Sarah also continued in her hospitality to family friends, church members, and her husband's pastoral colleagues, with Samuel Hopkins of Great Barrington being a regular guest in their home.

The tragedies of the year 1757 brought exceptional change to the entire Edwards family. Esther's husband Aaron Burr died suddenly of smallpox, and Jonathan Edwards was named to replace him as president of the College of New Jersey. Almost immediately Jonathan Edwards left Stockbridge for Newark to comfort his daughter and to prepare for his new responsibilities, only to arrive in the midst of an epidemic of the virulent disease. Left at home to pack the household, Sarah, who was grieving her daughter's great loss, was notified of her own husband's death in March 1758. William Schippen, the doctor who inoculated Jonathan Edwards with the smallpox vaccine, wrote to inform Sarah that her husband died from the disease. Mother and daughter were allied in their shared sorrow, and Sarah Edwards took the opportunity to write to her daughter about the comforts that Christian belief holds for the widow:

O my very Dear Child

What shall I say. A holy and Good God heas cover'd us with Dark Cloud. O that we may all kiss the rod and Lay our hands on our mouthes. The Lord heas Done it. He heas made me adore his goodness that we had him so Long. But my God Lives and he heas my heart. O what A Legacy my Husband and your Father heas Left us. We are all given to God and their I am and Love to be.

Sarah Edwards[23]

Tragedy upon tragedy, Esther Edwards Burr died within a month of her father, which necessitated newly widowed Sarah's immediate move to Newark to care for her orphaned grandchildren, Sally and Aaron, Jr. In keeping with the way she had comported herself throughout her life, Sarah rose to this challenge. She collected her daughter's babies, and while caring for them and comforting them, she too was stricken with illness. Sarah Pierpont Edwards contracted dysentery and survived her husband by only six months. She died in October 1758.

Deborah Prince, the English-born wife of Rev. Thomas Prince, was a close friend of Sarah Pierpont Edwards throughout life.[24] Thomas was a Harvard graduate and a ministerial colleague of Jonathan Edwards. The two couples, both with growing families, enjoyed each other's company. On numerous occasions Thomas Prince assisted Edwards with his publication projects, and Prince supported the controversial Edwards personally and professionally throughout Edwards's volatile ministerial career.

Sarah Prince was the fourth of their five children. The oldest was a brother born in 1722, named after his father. Sisters Deborah and Mercy were born in 1723 and 1725, respectively, and Sarah followed in 1728. The youngest, a girl named Grace, died one week after her birth in 1743. When Sarah was born, her father was associate pastor to Dr. Joseph Sewall at Old South Church in Boston, and the family lived on Washington Street, in a large home where Gov. John Winthrop and his family had once resided. The Edwards family visited the Princes in this home, and these events marked the beginning of a girlhood friendship between the young Esther Edwards and Sarah Prince. Their friendship would mature and, much like their mothers' relationship, would endure throughout their lives.

The Prince family was more financially secure than most junior minister's families of the time, perhaps because of their sizable land holdings. In addition to being well educated, Thomas Prince was well traveled and was a dedicated bibliophile. Sarah enjoyed her father's extensive library and benefited from access to the wide range of books; these were circumstances that she appreciated as both felicitous and exceptional. In a recollection of her childhood, the library is prominent among the blessings she recounts: "I praise my Bountyfull Lord for the Distinguishing helps he affords me (beyond allmost any of my Age and Sex) of Divine knowledge and christian Piety. For such a Father, such Ministers, such a sister [and] such Books as he favoured me with. How can I be Eno' Thankfull!"[25]

Religion and literature at the center of her life, Sarah Prince was convinced very early of the importance of keeping a spiritual diary. In 1743, at the age of fifteen during the height of the Great Awakening, she read John White's *The Power of Godliness*, which emphasized the value of recording one's spiritual development.[26] Sarah Prince Gill's narrative spans twenty-one years. An educated and accomplished member of Boston society, Sarah Prince is known to today's reader primarily as "Fidelia," her nom de plume as a member of Esther Edwards Burr's epistolary circle.[27] Although they lived a considerable distance apart, Sarah in Boston and Esther in Newark, following her marriage to Aaron Burr, the two women maintained their close ties through their correspondence. Indeed Esther Edwards Burr refers to her friend as "the Sister of my heart."[28] In her correspondence with Esther, Sarah Prince shows herself to be well read, articulate, interested in all things cultural, and committed to spiritual self-examination and growth. Although their letters provide detailed news of family, friends, and domestic life, the correspondents are most impassioned when they express their religious concerns.

While Sarah Prince's spiritual narrative and her correspondence with Esther Edwards Burr illustrate her broad literary interests and her fascination with the world of ideas in general, they also reveal her disinterest in domestic pursuits. This is perhaps one reason why she mentions her mother so infrequently; she was simply not engaged by her mother's interests and activities. This may also explain her relatively late marriage, at the age of thirty-one, to Moses Gill. Moses Gill was five years her junior, a successful merchant who rose from an otherwise modest background. They had no children, and Sarah Gill mentions her husband only once in her narrative: "It having pleased God in his sovereign Providence to bring me into a Marriage Union on Mar 27 with one who I Esteem As a Person hopefully Pious and has made me the head of a family" (76).

The decision to marry must have been a longstanding and vexing concern for Sarah Prince. Aaron Burr, Sr. suggests as much in a letter he wrote to the young woman in 1753, in which he alludes to concerns that she had expressed earlier:

> As to your . . . Inference: about Women's loosing their Brains upon marrying, we are willing it should stand as it is. But it [. . .] a Word of Encouragement to those Ladies that cant find Gentlemen of equal Brains to themselves to marry however, in Hopes there will be a Balance afterward.
>
> As to the last Query—Whether Men's increase in Proportion to the Decrease of the Women's I beg leave to reply—That if the Gentleman that married you don't find his to increase Twill be a plain Evidence he had none before.[29]

Clearly Sarah Prince's investment in her intellectual life and her reputation as a learned woman were among her personal obstacles to early marriage. Ultimately, although she expresses no real joy in her married life to Moses Gill, the alliance afforded her leisure to read, write, and continue her correspondence with the remaining members of the female epistolary circle that she and Esther Edwards Burr once termed the "Sisterhood."

Because so many family members and friends died in the decade before her marriage, one might also speculate that Sarah Prince never felt the desire for marital companionship until she found herself quite alone in the world. Her last remaining sister, Mercy, died in 1752, and then in 1757 Aaron Burr was stricken with smallpox. The following year saw the deaths of Esther Edwards Burr and Sarah Prince's father. It is perhaps significant that there are no entries in her journal for five months following her meditations on her father's death on October 22, 1758. The next entry on March 25, 1759, announces dryly that she will marry in two day's time.

Moses Gill, Esq., served as one of the judges of the county court of common pleas as well as counselor of the Commonwealth of Massachusetts. He was an exceptionally prosperous man, and he and Sarah were among the founding residents of Princeton, Massachusetts, where they established their home on a vast estate that exceeded three thousand acres. Their property consisted of an elegant mansion house, a farmhouse, a coach and chaise house, and a large barn. One of the special charms of the property was its hilltop placement. From the mansion's portico, one could see as far as Milton and the Boston Harbor.

Moses and Sarah had no children. Consequently, unlike Sarah Pierpont Edwards and Esther Edwards Burr, she had a minimum of domestic distractions. Sarah Prince Gill outlived her parents, all of her siblings, and her dear friend, Esther Burr. She died on August 5, 1771, at the age of forty-three, leaving Moses a widower who subsequently remarried and remained in Princeton until his death in 1800.

The spiritual narratives of both Sarah Pierpont Edwards and Sarah Prince Gill exhibit many of the conventions of the Calvinist conversion narratives that were produced in New England in the seventeenth and eighteenth centuries.[30] At the same time, these accounts are also inflected by gender and, as such, add to our understanding of women's experience of religion. Finally the historical context of the two narratives—one authored in 1742 and the other from 1743 until 1764—is important in understanding the texts themselves, as well as the shift in religious thought from the period of the Great Awakening until the threshold of the nineteenth century.

The Cambridge Platform of 1648 was clear in its recommendation of a narrative of one's conversation and found that "a personall and publick confession, and declaring of God's manner of working upon the soul, is both lawfull, expedient, and usefull, in sundry respects and upon sundry gounds."[31] Thomas Shepard was one of the earliest ministers in the seventeenth-century Massachusetts Bay Colony to articulate prescriptions for the Calvinist conversion narrative. The prominent minister and author directed his Cambridge congregation to produce spiritual journals that expressed more than a catalog of their sins or a celebration of their spiritual joys. According to Shepard, the narrative of one's path to grace should offer such [accounts] as may be of special use unto the people of God, such things as tend to shew, Thus I was humbled, then thus I was called, then thus I have walked, though with many weaknesses since, and such special providences of God I have seen, temptations gone through, and thus the Lord hath delivered me, blessed be his Name, etc.[32]

Thus Shepard attempted to codify the genre in ways that emphasize the dramatic development of the convert as a direct result of the transformative nature of free grace. Edmund Morgan, one of the earliest critics to investigate this form of spiritual narrative, outlines the morphology of conversion as the initial recognition of human depravity, followed by submission of the will to God's authority, knowledge and acceptance of God's law, and awareness of one's own sin, which is termed "conviction" or "humiliation." These preparatory stages anticipate a spiritual battle in which the soul struggles with despair and yearns for God's saving grace. Ultimately the convert becomes profoundly aware of God's assurance of justification, which William Ames defines as "the gracious judgment of God by which he absolves the believer from sin and death, and reckons him righteous and worthy of life for the sake of Christ."[33] Justification then manifests itself in virtuous behavior and in sanctification, by which the penitent is "vivified" and restored to the image and life of God.[34]

The exceptional experience of receiving God's grace is not a singular event in a Christian's life. Rather, conversion is the identification of regeneration that marks the beginning of a life of spiritual introspection and subsequent deepening experiences of grace. Charles E. Hambrick-Stowe finds that the later experiences follow the pattern of the original recognition of conversion, and he cites Thomas Shepard, who speaks of his spiritual maturity in terms of "renewed conversions."[35] Thus, for the regenerate Christian, the earliest conviction of conversion will engender a series of increasingly profound experiences of the reception of grace throughout life. Likewise the renewed awareness of grace may be anticipated by an equally acute sense of personal depravity and then may again spawn a more penetrating awareness of one's depravity, the full cycle of conversion expressing the continuing maturation of the Christian's relationship with God. Consequently the regenerate Christian is charged with perpetual introspection concerning the path of the soul to God because this task does not end with the initial experience of grace. For the mature Christian, written accounts of one's spiritual growth may then indeed include elements of the conversion narrative, the believer's life evincing a series of "renewed conversions."

When Thomas Shepard wrote that the conversion narrative "may be of special use unto the people of God," he was mindful of the didactic mission of the convert's narrative itself. The unregenerate would learn by the example of the newly regenerate, and the members of the congregation would hear their religious tenets rearticulated and thus reaffirmed by the testimony of the convert. Their personal paths to God and their collective mission as a community of believers are rehearsed once again in the words of the new member of the congregation.

Both Shepard and his ministerial colleague John Cotton worked toward institutionalizing the conversion narrative. Cotton, minister of the First Church of Boston and renowned author, insisted that an oral relation of one's regeneration before the congregation must be a requirement for full church membership.[36]

Almost a century later, after the practice of the oral relation had been largely abandoned, Jonathan Edwards would concur with the early Puritan divines, Thomas Shepard and John Cotton, and the 1648 Cambridge Platform: "There is no one thing I know of, that God has made such a means of promoting his work amongst us, as the news of others' conversion[s]."[37] In his reformation of church government, Edwards attempted to revive the requirement of a personal and "credible" statement of conversion for admission to church membership, this being a central point of contention with his congregation.[38] Consistent with his practice, Jonathan Edwards led by example. He authored a statement of his regeneration, "A Personal Narrative," which he shared with Aaron Burr, the divinity student who would become his son-in-law, for the purpose of instructing and encouraging Burr's spiritual growth. He also made use of Sarah Edwards's renewed conversion in 1742 as model and inspiration for the people of New England when he disseminated his narrative of this experience as part of his tract *Some Thoughts Concerning the Present Revival of Religion.*

Rodger Payne's 1998 study of American Protestant accounts of spiritual rebirth demonstrates the critical importance of oral relations in the development of the complex rhetorical conventions of the conversion narrative. Payne notes that

[b]ecause evangelicalism recognized—and even demanded— that converts should be able to offer a testimony of their experiences, conversion within the evangelical community became a

function of language. Only by appropriating the rhetoric and interpretive strategies that had been legitimated and sanctioned by the larger "interpretive community" was the experience of the individual validated. The idealized model of evangelical conversion—what might be termed the "text" of conversion—did not exist as some ethereal authority that was imposed upon individual autobiographers, but was in fact constantly created by the individuals within the evangelical community.[39]

The linguistic and literary features of the idealized master narrative that are only partially realized in the individual accounts include scriptural reference and self-identification with biblical figures as well as the posture of inadequacy to express the abject self. Invariably such narratives express the penitent's recognition of an inability to effect one's salvation and acknowledgment that God's grace creates the glorified self. The plot structure is ascendant, but it also illustrates the dramatic reversals that reflect the inevitable human regression. These rhetorical conventions have sometimes been perceived as tiresome perhaps because readers misinterpret and undervalue their critical function for both the self and the community. Indeed the role of the community of believers complicates the production of the narrative of religious experience. It must be recognized that the new convert addresses both God and human in the conversion narrative, the human being the collective church membership. When the posture of the penitent is simultaneously one of mortification before the deity and humility before the congregation, then the convert is able to speak only because of the grace of God and then because of the specific language that the community of believers has made available. In a parallel movement of this ritual, the community too is validated by witnessing its own narrative enacted yet again.

The rhetoric of the eighteenth-century spiritual narrative invariably retains many of the qualities of the oral relation of one's conversion in the absence of the early oral requirement. It mirrors the plot, rhetorical figures, scriptural referents, and awareness of its dual audience of the earlier documents. Thus, when Sarah Pierpont Edwards opens her spiritual narrative, which is an account of a renewed conversion occurring decades after her first conversion, she begins, as did many penitents before her, with an acute sense of her depravity.[40] She writes, "On Tuesday night, Jan. 19, 1742, I felt very uneasy and unhappy, at my being so low in grace. I thought I very much needed help from God, and found a spirit of earnestness to seek help of him, that I might have more holiness" (1). This statement begins the cycle of mortification, submission to God's will, and ensuing glorification that frequently gives structure to both oral and written conversion narratives. Edwards's account is not linear but expresses the constant struggle with the state of one's soul in this world.

When the plot is in the descendent mode, Sarah Pierpont Edwards casts herself as "low." However, as one who has previously been assured of God's

Portrait of Mrs. Jonathan (Sarah Pierpont) Edwards by Joseph Badger, oil on canvas, a bequest of Eugene Phelps Edwards. Reprinted with permission of the Yale University Art Gallery.

saving grace, she would recognize this as a reassuring mark of Christian awareness. When the plot is in the ascendant mode, Sarah's spiritual narrative expresses her immense joy in the knowledge of the presence of God in her life, and the intimacy of her relationship with God. She characterizes God as her father, and she as his child. Early in her narrative, she asks, "Can I now at this time, with the confidence of a child, and without the least misgiving of heart, call God my Father?" (2). Later, she feels free to assert her standing as a child of God, whom God has "weaned" from the things of this world, and who is now watched by the "eye of God." In this way she also binds herself to her community when she identifies the entire congregation as children of God, all forming the body of God. In addition Edwards states that God the Father and God the Son appear to her as being "distinct persons," so she casts her relationship with Jesus Christ differently. "He was mine and I his," she writes. In direct allusion to the Song of Solomon, she characterizes her relationship with Christ in sensual terms. Christ appears to her, takes her heart, and puts it at his feet. She seeks his smile and perceives a "constant flowing and reflowing of heavenly and divine love, from Christ's heart to mine" (8).

The language of physical sensation is prominent throughout Edwards's spiritual narrative. This language is especially remarkable because her images of the rising and falling of her religious affections are not exclusively metaphorical. Although she speaks of a "silent and soft communion" with God, her religious experience is powerfully vocal, dramatic, intensely physical, and at times violent (2). While listening to a hymn, Sarah Edwards recounts "my soul was drawn so powerfully towards Christ and heaven, that I leaped unconsciously from my chair" (7). Alternatively, when she reflects on the depraved condition of mankind, "my strength was immediately taken away, and I sunk down on the spot. Those who were near raised me, and placed me in a chair" (7). In these instances Edwards's body symbolically reflects the specific state of her affections. In others she is simply overcome by the sense of divine working in her soul such that she weeps openly or loses all control of her body: "the consciousness I had of the reality and the excellence of heavenly things was so clear, and the affections they excited so intense, that it overcame my strength, and kept my body weak and faint, the great part of the day, so that I could not stand or go without help" (14).

Many conversion narratives and other forms of spiritual narratives in this and earlier periods rely on metaphors of the depth of one's depravity and the height of one's glory. New converts predictably speak figuratively of groveling in the dirt at the feet of the Lord or sensing a newfound light-ness such that they might soar to the heavens. Edwards's claim that "I seemed to dwell on high" is clearly metaphorical (3). However, her account of bodily response demonstrates the affective and even physical nature of the evangelical experience of regeneration, an aspect of religious life that her husband was early to recognize.[41]

The term "regeneration" itself is a metaphor that insists on the new spiritual life of a Christian convert. The sinful self dies, and the saintly self is born in Christ.[42] Because of the physicality of Sarah Pierpont Edwards's spiritual narrative, her language not only relays these tropes—she models the death of the penitent. She reports the sensation of her soul leaving the body, leaping toward the heavens, this image consistent with earlier con-version narratives. Moreover, she speaks of losing physical strength, her flesh becoming cold, and her neighbors laying her on the bed, as if she were already a corpse.

Similarly language fails her. As Sarah struggles to characterize her physical sensations, as well as her lamentations and joys, she frequently admits that language is inadequate to describe her experience.[43] It is "inexpressible" and "unspeakable." Yet, she finds linguistic resources in the "instinctive language of [her] soul," which leads her to the word of God, scripture (5). Many of Sarah Edwards's emotional outbursts and physical paroxysms result from hearing a passage from the Bible, and she responds in kind, by repeating the word of God or speaking in language that is dense with scriptural allusions and scriptural metaphor. At times she engages in dialogue that is direct quotation or paraphrase of scripture. In this way she avails herself of words and figures at the very center of Christianity to assert her awareness of her identity as a Christian.

New to American spiritual narratives is Sarah Edwards's invocation of popular culture—hymnody and religious poetry. Jonathan Edwards had recently consented to his congregation's singing hymns during church services, and in her spiritual narrative Sarah Edwards exhibits her strong attachment to these works. Instead of quoting scripture, she frequently offers Isaac Watts's version of a psalm or Elizabeth Singer Rowe's medita-tional verse inspired by a biblical passage.[44] Sarah was so taken with John Mason's variant of the Magnificat that she continued to repeat his words several days afterward.[45] Her persistent reference to these popular works signals their acceptance as worthy of Christian meditation. Moreover, her invocation of these popular materials is evidence of the plasticity of Cal-vinist spiritual narratives; they are dynamic and individual.

Sarah's spiritual narrative progresses chronologically, which might suggest that it is neatly structured. However, this is far from the case. She recounts the events of the two-week period in fits and starts, blurring days and nights. This is consistent with the ecstatic tone of Sarah's narrative in which she breathlessly intones a phrase from scripture, moves quickly to describe her lifeless limbs, characterizes a conversation, then repeats the scripture almost as a coda. Hymns are juxtaposed with dialogue, and poetry is mixed with prayer. Throughout, her narration is phrased in highly charged language that speaks alternately in superlatives and negatives, stylistic markers that reveal her heightened awareness of both her regeneration and depravity.

An opposing narrative feature, one of the most consistent and regular aspects of her work, is her documentation of her community. Sarah recalls, for example, which minister's remark elicited her emotional response, which individuals attended evening prayer at her home, which man from the congregation conversed with her, and which woman noticed her physical condition. Society is meticulously chronicled.

To frame her discussion of her fellow men and women, the account draws on conventional, religious phrasings in expressing love for humanity and union with the community of believers within the metaphorical body of Christ. At the same time, it reveals Sarah Edwards's exceptional understanding of the social imperative of spiritual regeneration.[46] She writes, "I realized also, in an unusual and very lively manner, how great a part of Christianity lies in the performance of our social and relative duties to one another" (13). Although the object of this tract is to document her individual spiritual growth, one of its central themes is her desire for the workings of the Holy Spirit in Northampton. Indeed Edwards clearly understands her spiritual aspirations for her congregation to be an essential condition of her regeneration. This awareness is in part consonant with Payne's analysis of the communal nature of the rhetoric of conversion. Her heightened and overt claims on this theme also stem from her awareness of her standing as the minister's wife and the position of *exemplum fidei* that this leadership position implies—indeed demands.

However, any statement about Sarah Pierpont Edwards's religious mission within her home, the village, or the Northampton church congregation is complicated. That is, Edwards begins her narrative by revealing that she is acutely affected by "the ill treatment of the town, and the ill will of my husband" (3). According to Sarah, Jonathan Edwards had reproached her for lacking "prudence" in conversation with Chester

Williams, a neighboring minister who had engaged in longstanding theological disagreements with Jonathan Edwards (1).[47] The congregation
too was increasingly disaffected with the minister's wife and was often at
odds with the minister. At the time when she documented that she had
experienced this exceptional outpouring of God's affection, she was
alone. Her husband was summoned to preach in Leicester and would be
away for two full weeks, a fact that she mentions several times in her narrative. While visiting ministers, including a young, talented, new Yale
graduate, Samuel Buell, took Jonathan Edwards's place in preaching to his
church, Sarah Edwards became the spousal representative of her husband's ministry in Northampton.[48] Acting as gracious hostess to those
who might replace her husband in the affections of the congregation, she
was also advocating for his merit in his absence.[49]

Sarah Edwards admits that she cannot enjoy the peace of the Lord
because of her concern for her reputation in Northampton and her husband's treatment by his congregation. Then, when Sarah quotes from Ralph
Erskine's poem "The Valour and Victories of Faith," she offers some insight into her complex frame of mind. She selects two of the most gentle-
hearted lines of the poem to represent her thoughts:

> I see him lay his vengeance by,
> And smile in Jesus' face.[50]

However, as she well knows, these lines are atypical of the poem. The
prominent theme of the eighty-line poem is the terrible, avenging power
afforded by God's grace. More specifically, Erskine argues that God will
smite those who harm his children:

> By faith I have a conqu'ring pow'r
>   To tread upon my foes,
> To triumph in a dying hour,
>   And banish all my woes.

And

> By faith I counterplot my foes,
>   Nor need their ambush fear;
> Because my life-guard also goes
>   Behind me in the rear.[51]

Although Sarah Edwards quotes two mild lines that speak of the vengeful
God whose heart is softened on behalf of those who have received Jesus'

saving grace, the backdrop of these lines is that God will then turn his wrath against the enemies of his elect. Sarah Edwards is looking to God to protect her and her husband's standing in Northampton, by whatever means possible. Or, in Erskine's words, she will use her faith to counter-plot her foes.

Yet Sarah Edwards repeatedly asserts that God's love allows her to dismiss her husband's and the community's opinion of her. In an especially dramatic passage, she writes,

> There was then a deep snow on the ground, and I could think of being driven from my home into the cold and snow, of being chased from the town with the utmost contempt and malice, and of being left to perish with the cold, as cast out by all the world, with perfect calmness and serenity. It appeared to me, that it would not move me, or in the least disturb the inexpressible happiness and peace of my soul. My mind seemed as much above all such things, as the sun is above the earth. (3)

Edwards's detachment from her community appears to defy her almost simultaneous assertions of the social mission demanded of a Christian and of her delicate political position in Northampton. Likewise her physical movement throughout the narrative—in addition to the rise and fall of her emotions and her body—can be viewed as an advance followed by a retreat. That is, she alternately engages with the congregation and the visiting ministers, and then she deliberately withdraws.

However, this seemingly contradictory impulse is directly related to another dominant theme of her account: submission. Sarah Edwards recalls that her first evidence of her spiritual quickening was "great quietness of spirit, unusual submission to God, and willingness to wait upon him" (1). She reprises and rephrases this sentiment throughout her account as acquiescence and as resignation or resignedness. Likewise, when she finds herself groping for language, she frequently cries, "Amen, Lord Jesus! Amen, Lord Jesus," this too being an expression of ratification of and submission to God's word (5, 9, 12). Once she is perfectly subdued to the will of God to use her, her husband, and her community as he wishes, she no longer fears humiliation before men or even the pain of death. At this point Edwards's ethos shifts as she refashions herself as an instrument of God's desire on earth.

The implications of Sarah Edwards's reconstructed ethos are many. Primarily it affords her a way of asserting a communal identity. In the final moments recorded in her spiritual narrative, she speaks of being heartened by others' accounts of the influence of God in their lives such that she desires to "follow after them to heaven" (16).[52] In this way Sarah Edwards's posture of submission enables her to integrate herself into the church membership. It also permits her to reconcile her conviction of her election with her social mission. She models God's grace for the community, and she finds models of salvation in the sermons, hymns, poems, oral relations, and conversations within the community.

In a more strategic sense, this posture allows her to celebrate freely the success of the visiting ministers, as well as the accomplishments of her husband at home and away, because she casts these men as instruments too (4, 7, 9, 15). Her presentation of herself as God's humble, female steward does not deny her agency or authority precisely because of her simultaneous assertion of members of the ministry as humble, male stewards. In her new spiritual schema, they have equivalent standing.

Sarah Edwards's reading in popular culture again offers insight into a strategy for using faith to "counterplot" her foes. Sarah chose John Mason's meditation on the Magnificat for inclusion in her spiritual narrative, this scriptural passage celebrating God's selection of one woman for an exceptional position. In the Bible, when God elects Mary to be the mother of Jesus, she recognizes that her soul "doth magnify the Lord." As Sandra Gustafson has observed, "Mary provides Sarah with a model for female expressiveness that temporarily unites voice and gesture."[53] Enacting the unique relationship with God that Mary enjoys, Sarah assumes a special spiritual authority that is not only located outside of the traditional framework of masculine religious leadership, but also excludes the established, male ministry. In this way Sarah works to undermine those who might compromise her husband's position, and she redirects their attention to herself as the representative of Jonathan Edwards's ministry.

Mason's hymn also speaks of God's grace giving one authority to call him Father. Moreover, "It makes me cry, My Lord, my God, / And that without Controul." Sarah Edwards's language echoes that of the poem, but, perhaps more important, her ecstatic experience mirrors that of the poem's speaker. Both claim to exhibit God's grace, and as a result both call God's name without control and have the sensation of leaping and flying to the heavens. In this way Mason's verse offered Sarah a precise protocol of physically asserting her identity as an exceptional Christian woman who has been touched by God, the drama of which furthered her goal of drawing attention from her husband's rivals.

Thus Edwards' narrative situates its experience in the language of the congregation, as Payne has described this impulse, and at the same time addresses the politics of the community. Finding power in submission and expressing her heart in the language of others, her voice attempts to solidify the religious congregation not only in its covenant of faith with God, but also around its minister and its minister's model wife. That she enacted her experience of grace in the emotive mode that her evangelist husband advocated offered further support for Jonathan Edwards's position.

Gill's spiritual narrative begins in 1743, following Sarah Edwards's 1742 narrative, and ends in 1764. A historical complement to the earlier document, it offers the perspective of the next generation of Calvinist women, who came of age during the Great Awakening and whose religious orientation was also inflected by Enlightenment values. Whereas Edwards's account expresses its orthodox Calvinist training and affirms the social orientation of the woman in public life, Gill's can best be understood as enlightened evangelism, which bridges eighteenth-century Calvinism and later Protestant movements.[54] That is, Sarah Prince Gill's account illustrates the sometimes-uneasy assimilation of Enlightenment values into religious discourse.

Unlike Sarah Pierpont Edwards's narrative, which her husband expressly requested and then rewrote for public dissemination, Sarah Gill's account of her religious development is an exclusively private document. It shares many of the features of a personal journal in which she is simultaneously the author, subject, and audience of the text. Like Edwards, Gill had experienced early regeneration, but, as a vigilant Calvinist, she was continually alert to signs of flagging spirituality and likewise awaited any sign of a maturing relationship with God with a keen desire for the experience of a renewed conversion. Thus, in her spiritual narrative, Gill clearly attends to the discourse of the oral and written relations of conversion, which in part provide a pattern for her personal self-examination.

Early in the narrative, Gill takes stock of her spiritual life and outlines rather bluntly her estimation of her standing: "I would set myself in the presence of *God* to Examine with care and Deliveration [Deliberation] My self, whether I am the Subject of a Work of *Conviction, Convertion,* [and] *Sanctification,* 1st Original Sin, actual sin, Indwelling sin, and think I find as follows" (24). This passage and Gill's subsequent analysis of the presence of grace in her life identify the goal of her exercise as both documentation

and self-assessment. These sections likewise look to a much-desired renewed experience of God's grace.

Here and elsewhere she articulates her intellectual acceptance of the
Calvinist understanding of the condition of humanity and God's law: "I see
it to be Just in God to impute [Adam's] sin to him and his posterity," and

The Portrait of Sarah Prince Gill by John Singleton Copley, oil on canvas, a bequest of the Jesse Metcalf Fund. Reprinted with permission of the
Museum of Art, Rhode Island School of Design. Photograph of Copley's
painting by Del Bogart.

"I have been brought to see . . . that it was Just in God to condemn me to Eternal Missery" (24, 25). Assertions of doctrinal belief or confessions of difficulty in accepting church tenets are common to many variants of spiritual narratives, conversion narratives among them. In seventeenth-century New England, Anne Bradstreet confesses her struggle with sectarianism and even admits that on many occasions she has questioned "the verity of the Scriptures."[55] A century later Jonathan Edwards's "Personal Narrative" reveals his "objections against the doctrine of God's sovereignty, in choosing whom he would to eternal life, and rejecting whom he pleased," which he found to be a "horrible doctrine."[56] Whereas Gill signals her agreement with specific articles of faith, she does not disclose difficulties in understanding or accepting doctrine.

Gill's particular spiritual conflict concerns her attachment to the world and its pleasures. In fact she claims that she would prefer an intellectual variance with God's law to her emotional struggle.

> I find no living near to God with out much . . . Prayer and Meditation and strict watching—Otherways Carnality will grow upon me—I think sometimes I had rather endure those terrible Conflicts than this Indifferancy—Conflicts produce Fear, watchfulness, etc., but this is a Monster portion in Many Sins and Desertions—O wretched sinfull heart! (56)

Throughout the twenty-one years documented in her writing, Gill consistently confesses her "passion over *worldly carefulness*, the Bane of Godliness" and struggles with "natural inclinations" (83, 61). Of her "Weaknesses," she admits that she is especially drawn to idle, social conversation, concerns herself with the "Applause or Cencure of Mortals," and suffers too keenly from perceived slights from other women (62).[57]

Similar to many Calvinist conversion narratives, Sarah Gill's account responds to specific passages and at times individual words from scripture. To characterize her prose as replete with biblical quotation and dense with scriptural allusion is to understate her linguistic reliance on scriptural themes, plots, and metaphors. Like Sarah Edwards, she is fully fluent in the language of the Bible, such that the language of the Bible shapes her experience of self. Thus, when Gill grieves the death of her friend Esther Edwards Burr and writes that Esther was the "Apple of my Eye," she is using not only a popular figure of speech, but also an allusion to the interdicted fruit of the tree of the knowledge of good and evil, which anticipates her observation that "My God hides his Face!" (72).

Sarah Gill also draws on the spiritual texts of her historical moment—sermons, hymns, religious poetry, and other religious writing. In fact John White's *New England's Lamentations*, with its message of the value of chronicling one's religious development, provided the impetus for her spiritual autobiography (17). Most frequently she uses religious literature as inspiration to overcome her persistent worldliness. For example, she notes that Owen's tract *Phronema to pneumatos; or, The grace and duty of being spiritually-minded* provides her with motivation to "bring my heart to a strict Scrutiny," and she senses that a sermon on Proverbs 4:23 speaks directly to the condition of her soul (57–58, 83).[58] Indeed she is so taken with the encouragement provided by Elizabeth Singer Rowe's popular *Devout Exercises of the Heart* that these writings become the model for her religious meditation; at times she replicates much of Rowe's phrasings or simply copies Rowe's meditations outright in her journal (31–32, 50, 84–85).

This is not to suggest that Sarah Prince Gill merely apes the thoughts and words of others. In a larger sense Gill must necessarily employ these materials to express the inexpressible self. Throughout her narrative she searches for language and finds herself inadequate to speak, and she insists on the poverty or negation of language: "Language can't describe my then Views" and "I am Vile, and I cou'd not express how Vile" (16, 41).[59] When the requisite posture of the penitent is the inability to act or speak except through the will of God, spiritual narrative evinces the linguistic implications of this stance. Thus the author often relies on the word of the Bible or the language of the community of believers as a vehicle for self-expression. Gill addresses the premise of this impulse: "O, I long'd to have no Will of my own but to have his Will my settled choice and from thence to have it the genuine Language of my heart" (46–47). She also gives evidence of the practice of seeking language in the word of God: "I hope God was nearer to me this day than for a long Season. He has been moving on the Face of the Waters, yea, stirring up the waters of the Sanctu-ary for my healing. He enabled me to Cry for a suitable Word, and he sent me a Word in season from Revelation 2:4, 5" (83). The inarticulate first sentence of this passage is quickly replaced by a second that is informed by images and metaphors from the psalms. Emphasizing her passive position, Gill then prays for language to express the self, when God alone effects the act of prayer itself. Ultimately she is offered a model language found in scripture. Repeatedly characterizing her power of speech as "grones," language becomes choate and vital when it echoes the word of God.

Rodger Payne has identified a critical tension inherent in writing the self within the framework of Calvinist conversion, that is, the self-definition that accompanies such narratives: "The language of conversion pressed them to speak of self-annihilation," he notes, "but in speaking thus they counteracted the very intent of such discourse."[60] This is an aspect of Gill's spiritual narrative as well. Although this tension is miti-gated by her reliance on the language of scripture, sermons, hymns, and other religious writing, Sarah Prince Gill's Enlightenment values further complicate her posture of absolute humility. Invoking conventional tropes, she characterizes herself as a "poor worm," a "Nothing Worm," and, more eloquently, a "barren Fig tree," and she further acknowledges that she "never saw more clearly that I can do nothing, but since Christ has promised to work in me to Will and to do (and that of his meer Grace) I chuse to labor in his strength, to Work out my salvation with Fear, etc." (38, 44, 27, 47). Although Gill assumes the posture of self-annihilation, she nonetheless asserts the role of her intellect in guiding the spirit toward salvation. When she is spiritually lifeless, she speaks of being "stupid," claims that "my reason was clouded," and cries, "O, my Stupidity scares me!" (33, 68).

Correspondingly she understands her movement toward God as a personal choice that issues from the individual mind and the will. Gill insists on her agency in making a choice in her salvation, and the very word "choice" is invoked continually throughout her narrative. Interrogating herself, she writes, "Again, Pause, Consider Well, and then answer, Which is thy free, full, deliberate, serious choice? . . . I have made choice of God for my Portion" (35). Consistent with the language of rational decisions, in the same entry Sarah Prince Gill offers a chart to illustrate clearly the distinctions between spiritual and worldly attractions (34). At times she employs self-designed, rigid protocols for her meditation and prayer and suggests that the intellectual exercise of adhering to her structured process is beneficial (42–43, 80–81). Religion is a "duty," religious observance is a function of the "will," and religious faith is a matter of "choice." Likewise, in Sarah Gill's rational approach to her spiritual life, God is characterized metaphorically as her "Vital head in all things" (43).

Rodger Payne has observed the "ambivalence of self" in nineteenth-century evangelical autobiographers for whom the understanding of conversion as a personal decision runs counter to the humiliation and annihilation. He writes, "In their conversion narratives and spiritual auto-biographies, evangelical authors often commented upon the array of choices that confronted them, including . . . the ability to accept or reject grace and conversion."[61] Gill's narrative is an early expression of the role of the mind and will in one's experience of religion.

Yet, here again, the enlightened evangelist is conflicted. Sarah Prince Gill recognizes the limitations of her ability to reason and to choose. At the close of her program of religious exercise on October 4, 1763, she observes that she could "pray and spread my spiritual Mallady before God with more Freedom than before." However, she also expresses her distrust of this process: "Was help'd to Some Sincerity. I hope 'twas not wholly Formal, tho' alass, too much. . . . I look'd to God for direction to make *proper resolutions* and at Length came to this: *to spend a Day in this way as often as* [. . .] *my Family duties will allow*" (88). Thus, while Gill believes her process to be productive, she nonetheless regularly questions the efficacy of her structure and seeks divine wisdom to guide and authorize human agency.

Adhering to reason, Gill does not deny her passion. Indeed she invokes both impulses simultaneously, avowing that "my soul cleaves to [God] with Unshaken desire and choice" (65). She looks to the Lord to "enlightn [her] in the Knowledge of his Will and Way," but she also seeks to "know the Love of Christ which passeth knowledge" (19, 29). In her September 12, 1756, entry, after chastening herself for sensuality, which binds her to the things of this world, she nonetheless denigrates the role of reason in fostering her spiritual development and yearns for an affective and aesthetic experience of her religion: "Let me see the King in his Beauty, and that will captivate my whole soul and do more towards sublimating My affections in one Moment than the most rational arguments and persuasive reasonings, the pomp of Rhetoric, and flow of Eloquence cou'd do in a thousand Years" (38). Gill returns to her deliberation, debate, lists, and methods but is not blind to the inadequacy of rationalism in her spiritual pursuits.

The style of Gill's prose points to this tension between sense and sensibility. On one hand, the text is guided by her attention to process. She notes the four biblical passages to which she currently attends, lists the five concerns about which she prays, articulates the four reasons that she hopes for salvation, includes a chart that contrasts vices and virtues, and chronicles her day—prayer by prayer, hymn by hymn. In opening statements such as "This day was spent as designed in the Following Method," the double articulation of process correctly predicts the tenor of the remaining prose for this entry (87). At times, however, her work contains many of the features of the emotive language that characterize Sarah Edwards's narrative: hyperbole, ejaculation, repetition, redundancy, and ruptured syntax. In the later work the emotional gestures are clearly tempered by Gill's insistence on method.

One goal of Sarah Prince Gill's spiritual narrative is to understand the temporal and spiritual limitation of the world and to live in a way that values and anticipates the eternal life that is promised. Similar to the writing of Sarah Pierpont Edwards, Gill's narrative often frames the relationship with God in worldly terms, using the language that describes intimate human alliances. Some of these tropes are scriptural, familiar, and familial: where God is father, the author is the child, and where God is husband, the author is the bride. Gill additionally speaks of God in hierarchical terms as her "King," "Conqueror," and the "captain of my salvation" but also more intimately as her "Abba, Father" and "Chosen and only Sure Friend" (40, 70).[62]

If Sarah Prince Gill is anxious about her affection for the world, her sense of social mission—like that of Sarah Pierpont Edwards—is an outcome of this affection. She speaks of her personal commitment to observing the "golden rule," and within her home she feels the burden of her responsibility for the Christian education and comportment of her servants (76). In a larger sense Gill desires Christian salvation for all people. In her words, "I wanted all to tast[e] and see that God is Good" (18). In her prayer Gill regularly pleads on behalf of a virtual catalog of individuals and institutions, which in one entry includes

> My Particular Friends—All in Affliction [and] Temptation, [also] The Town—Its churches—Its Ministers, The Land, its Ministers, churches, Magistrates, Lord Loudon—The Nation, The King—all his Ministers of state, Parliament, Officers, all his subjects, the church, Mr Whitefield, the Protestant Nations—Poor Protestants in France and Else-where—The whole church Militant—Yea, all the World and for the reign of Christ on Earth. (43)

That Gill cites the church multiple times within this one statement signals her special concern about her particular congregation. Her church was without a minister after her father's death in 1758 until 1760, when it appointed a minister who was unable to unify the congregation on a number of critical issues. If one of the functions of Calvinist spiritual narrative is to bind the penitent with a community of believers, the fractious nature of her congregation would have troubled her understanding of Christian identity. In December 1759, after spending "some times whole days in Prayer for that dear church," she laments the irregular religious services, and she concludes,

> God has been sore displeased with Us (as a church). We have left our first love, and he is forsaking of Us! I desire to lay low before him lamenting after him, bemoaning My sins, owning his Justice in the tokens of his Anger, and Our heinous sins as the procuring Cause of all. (77)

Because Gill conflates the self and the community, the state of her church calls into question the state of her soul. Gill's observations of discord in her church further vex her confidence in her ability to find peace in her heart and mind. Ultimately her fear that "God is about to break off Covenant with Us" carries a personal as well as communal significance for her (77). Although her spiritual narrative is a personal rather than a public document, she cannot avoid a consideration of public concerns. In fact the text asserts the unity of the believer with her religious community.

Finally the spiritual narratives of both Sarah Pierpont Edwards and Sarah Prince Gill are shaped in large part from the tension in their relationship to community. Profoundly religious, both women live in anticipation of the afterlife and profess to wean themselves from this world. The religious quickening of each woman takes place within a private, domestic locus. Yet this should not suggest that the experience lacks public dimension. Edwards and Gill are intimately tied to their religious community; their positions as church members and communicants were intensified by Edwards's status as minister's wife and minister's daughter and by Gill's as minister's daughter. Moreover both evince a fervent commitment to evangelism and the social mission of Christianity.

More important, both women express great anxiety about their voices within the community.[63] Sarah Edwards knows that her husband's congregation scrutinizes her every word, and she does not want to compromise his already-tenuous position. She claims too that her husband had complained of her conversation with a rival minister. Therefore she feels an obligation to check her voice until her husband urges her to proclaim herself to him and the public through her autobiographical spiritual narrative. In this way Sarah Pierpont Edwards is authorized by God, her minister, and her husband to assume a public voice on both private and public matters. Likewise Sarah Prince Gill is discomforted by social conversation. She feels demeaned and finds that her companions are diminished in their chatter. Gill redirects her language toward conversation with God and conversation with herself about the condition of her soul. In this way she can speak to the intimate, religious concerns that are prominent in her heart, and she also can address concerns about her community in a way that sanctifies her relationship to the world. Thus, through their authorship, Edwards and Gill are at liberty to express their private and public selves and to discover a means to fuse their lives in this world with their aspirations for eternity.

The implications of the Sarah Pierpont Edwards and Sarah Prince Gill's "silent and soft communion" with God are far-reaching. At some distance from the silent and soft, they are resounding and dramatic. Indeed the voice of the Calvinist woman in eighteenth-century America resonates far outside of her individual home and congregation such that her account influences women's narrative into the nineteenth century and beyond. In fact the spiritual narratives of eighteenth-century evangelical women represent a critical moment in female authorship. When women such as Sarah Pierpont Edwards and Sarah Prince Gill are encouraged to document their emotional and physical response to spiritual experience, the exploration of the female psychology and the female body is thus legitimized and even celebrated. Simultaneously women's authority to express the self and document the self in writing is also sanctioned and elevated. In this way the broad implications of conservative Calvinist spiritual narratives are ironically revolutionary and liberating. One can see that these public and private texts have an immediate and direct impact on the possibilities of female authorship even outside of a religious context just as they enrich the possibilities of female characterization within literary texts. No longer can women's experiences be reduced to binary categories as either spiritual or sensual, nor can women themselves be demeaned by binary characterization as either angelic or wanton. Eighteenth-century evangelism has liberated them to understand the unity of their spirituality and physicality and to speak of their intimate lives within a public framework.

It is not surprising then that Eliza Wharton in Hannah Webster Foster's late-eighteenth-century novel *The Coquette* uses much the same language as and similar arguments to those of Edwards and Gill to interrogate her desire and her duty. Likewise, in the nineteenth century, Mary Scudder in Harriet Beecher Stowe's *The Minister's Wooing* finds that she must acknowledge her physical passion in order to understand fully her role as a Christian wife, an understanding consonant with the religious and social experience of both Edwards and Gill. The meditative prose of Margaret Fuller's *Summer on the Lakes, in 1842* similarly exhibits the influence of the genre of the spiritual narrative. In many respects we can attribute the rise of female authorship in the late eighteenth and early nineteenth centuries in America to evangelical women's spiritual narratives in the eighteenth century. Encouraged to explore the self and then write about female experience, Sarah Pierpont Edwards and Sarah Prince Gill are models of Christian women authors who expose their intimate experience of religion in ways that are both conventional and novel. In a broader sense their narratives offer a rich portrait of female experience for generations of literary successors.

"The Comforter is come!"

The Spiritual Narrative of Sarah Pierpont Edwards

On Tuesday night, Jan. 19, 1742, I felt very uneasy and unhappy at my being so low in grace. I thought I very much needed help from God, and found a spirit of earnestness to seek help of him, that I might have more holiness. When I had for a time been earnestly wrestling with God for it, I felt within myself great quietness of spirit, unusual submission to God, and willingness to wait upon him, with respect to the time and manner in which he should help me, and wished that he should take his own time, and his own way, to do it.

The next morning, I found a degree of uneasiness in my mind, at Mr. Edwards's suggesting, that he thought I had failed in some measure in point of prudence, in some conversation I had with Mr. Williams of Hadley, the day before.[1] I found, that it seemed to bereave me of the quietness and calm of my mind, in any respect not to have the good opinion of my husband. This, I much disliked in myself, as arguing a want of a sufficient rest in God, and felt a disposition to fight against it, and look to God for his help, that I might have a more full and entire rest in him, independent of all other things. I continued in this frame, from early in the morning until about 10 o'clock, at which time the Rev. Mr. Reynolds went to prayer in the family.[2]

I had before this, so entirely given myself up to God, and resigned up every thing into his hands, that I had, for a long time, felt myself quite alone in the world; so that the peace and calm of my mind, and my rest in God, as my only and all sufficient happiness, seemed sensibly above the reach of disturbance from any thing but these two: 1st. My own good name and fair reputation among men, and especially the esteem and just treatment of the people of this town; 2dly. And more especially, the esteem, and love and kind treatment of my husband. At times, indeed, I had seemed to be considerably elevated above the influence of even these things; yet I had not found my calm, and peace and rest in God so sensibly, fully and constantly, above the reach of disturbance from them, until now.

While Mr. Reynolds was at prayer in the family this morning, I felt an earnest desire that, in calling on God, he should say, *Father*, or that he should address the Almighty under that appellation: on which the thought turned in my mind—*What can I say, Father?*—Can I now at this time, with the confidence of a child, and without the least misgiving of heart, call God my Father?—This brought to my mind, two lines of Mr. Erskine's Sonnet:

> "I see him lay his vengeance by,
> "And smile in Jesus' face."[3]

I was thus deeply sensible, that my sins did loudly call for vengeance; but I then by faith saw God "lay his vengeance by, and smile in Jesus' face." It appeared to be real and certain that he did so. I had not the least doubt, that he then sweetly smiled upon me, with the look of forgiveness and love, having laid aside all his displeasure towards me, for Jesus' sake; which made me feel very weak, and somewhat faint.

In consequence of this, I felt a strong desire to be alone with God, to go to him, without having any one to interrupt the silent and soft communion, which I earnestly desired between God and My own soul; and accordingly withdrew to my chamber. It should have been mentioned that, before I retired, while Mr. Reynolds was praying, these words, in Rom. 7:34, came into my mind *"Who is he that condemneth; It is Christ that died, yea rather that is risen again, who is even at the right hand of God, who also maketh intercession for us"*; as well as the following words, *"Who shall separate us from the love of Christ,"* etc.; which occasioned great sweetness and delight in my soul.[4] But when I was alone, the words came to my mind with far greater power and sweetness; upon which I took the Bible, and read the words to the end of the chapter, when they were impressed on my heart with vastly greater power and sweetness still. They appeared to me with undoubted certainty as the words of God, and as words which God did pronounce concerning me. I had no more doubt of it, than I had of my being. I seemed as it were to hear the great God proclaiming thus to the world concerning me; *"Who shall lay any thing to thy charge,"* etc.; and had it strongly impressed on me, how impossible it was for any thing in heaven or earth, in this world or the future, ever to separate me from the love of God which was in Christ Jesus.[5] I cannot find language to express, how *certain* this appeared—the everlasting mountains and hills were but shadows to it. My safety, and happiness, and eternal enjoyment of God's immutable love, seemed as durable and unchangeable as God himself. Melted and overcome by the sweetness of this assurance, I fell into a great flow of tears, and could not forbear weeping aloud. It appeared certain to me that God was my Father, and Christ my Lord and Saviour, that he was

2

mine and I his. Under a delightful sense of the immediate presence and love of God, these words seemed to come over and over in my mind, "My God, my all; my God, my all." The presence of God was so near, and so real, that I seemed scarcely conscious of any thing else. God the Father, and the Lord Jesus Christ, seemed as distinct persons, both manifesting their inconceivable loveliness and mildness, and gentleness, and their great and immutable love to me. I seemed to be taken under the care and charge of my God and Saviour, in an inexpressibly endearing manner; and Christ appeared to me as a mighty Saviour, under the character of the Lion of the Tribe of Judah, taking my heart, with all its corruptions, under his care, and putting it at his feet.[6] In all things, which concerned me, I felt myself safe under the protection of the Father and the Saviour; who appeared with supreme kindness to keep a record of every thing that I did, and of every thing that was done to me, purely for my good.

The peace and happiness, which I hereupon felt, was altogether inexpressible. It seemed to be that which came from heaven; to be eternal and unchangeable. I seemed to be lifted above earth and hell, out of the reach of every thing here below, so that I could look on all the rage and enmity of men or devils, with a kind of holy indifference, and an undisturbed tranquility. At the same time, I felt compassion and love for all mankind, and a deep abasement of soul, under a sense of my own unworthiness. I thought of the ministers who were in the house, and felt willing to undergo any labour and self-denial, if they would but come to the help of the Lord. I also felt myself more perfectly weaned from all things here below, than ever before. The whole world, with all its enjoyments, and all its troubles, seemed to be nothing:—My God was my all, my only portion.[7] No possible suffering appeared to be worth regarding: all persecutions and torments were a mere nothing. I seemed to dwell on high, and the place of defence to be the munition of rocks.

After some time, the two evils mentioned above, as those which I should have been least able to bear, came to my mind—the ill treatment of the town, and the ill will of my husband; but now I was carried exceedingly above even such things as these, and I could feel that, if I were exposed to them both, they would seem comparatively nothing. There was then a deep snow on the ground, and I could think of being driven from my home into the cold and snow, of being chased from the town with the utmost contempt and malice, and of being left to perish with the cold, as cast out by all the world, with perfect calmness and serenity. It appeared to me, that it would not move me, or in the least disturb the inexpressible happiness and peace of my soul. My mind seemed as much above all such things, as the sun is above the earth.

I continued in a very sweet and lively sense of divine things, day and night, sleeping and waking, until Saturday, January 23. On Saturday morning, I had a most solemn and deep impression on my mind of the eye of God as fixed upon me, to observe what improvement I made of those spiritual communications I had received from him; as well as of the respect shown Mr. Edwards, who had then been sent for to preach at Leicester. I was sensible that I was sinful enough to bestow it on my pride, or on my sloth, which seemed exceedingly dreadful to me. At night, my soul seemed to be filled with an inexpressibly sweet and pure love to God, and to the children of God; with a refreshing consolation and solace of soul, which made me willing to lie on the earth, at the feet of the servants of God, to declare his gracious dealings with me, and breathe forth before them my love, and gratitude and praise.

The next day, which was the Sabbath, I enjoyed a sweet, and lively and assured sense of God's infinite grace, and favour and love to me, in taking me out of the depths of hell, and exalting me to the heavenly glory, and the dignity of a royal priesthood.[8]

On Monday night, Mr. Edwards, being gone that day to Leicester, I heard that Mr. Buell was coming to this town, and from what I had heard of him, and of his success, I had strong hopes that there would be great effects from his labours here.[9] At the same time, I had a deep and affecting impression, that the eye of God was ever upon my heart, and that it greatly concerned me to watch my heart, and see to it that I was perfectly resigned to God, with respect to the instruments he should make use of to revive religion in this town, and be entirely willing, if it was God's pleasure, that he should make use of Mr. Buell; and also that other christians should appear to excel me in christian experience, and in the benefit they should derive from ministers. I was conscious, that it would be exceedingly provoking to God if I should not be thus resigned, and earnestly endeavoured to watch my heart, that no feelings of a contrary nature might arise; and was enabled, as I thought, to exercise full resignation, and acquiescence in God's pleasure, as to these things. I was sensible what great cause I had to bless God, for the use he had made of Mr. Edwards hitherto; but thought, if he never blessed his labours any more, and should greatly bless the labours of other ministers, I could entirely acquiesce in his will. It appeared to me meet and proper, that God should employ babes and sucklings to advance his kingdom.[10] When I thought of these things, it was my instinctive feeling to say, "Amen, Lord Jesus! Amen, Lord Jesus!" This seemed to be the sweet and instinctive language of my soul.

On Tuesday, I remained in a sweet and lively exercise of this resignation, and love to and rest in God, seeming to be in my heart from day to day, far above the reach of every thing here below. On Tuesday night, especially the latter part of it, I felt a great earnestness of soul and engagedness in seeking God for the town, that religion might now revive, and that God would bless Mr. Buell to that end. God seemed to be very near to me while I was thus striving with him for these things, and I had a strong hope that what I sought of him would be granted. There seemed naturally and unavoidably to arise in my mind an assurance, that now God would do great things for Northampton.

On Wednesday morning, I heard that Mr. Buell arrived the night before at Mr. Phelps's, and that there seemed to be great tokens and effects of the presence of God there, which greatly encouraged, and rejoiced me.[11] About an hour and a half after, Mr. Buell came to our house, I sat still in entire resignedness to God, and willingness that God should bless his labours here as much as he pleased; though it were to the enlivening of every saint, and to the conversion of every sinner, in the town. These feelings continued afterwards, when I saw his great success; as I never felt the least rising of heart to the contrary, but my submission was even and uniform, without interruption or disturbance. I rejoiced when I saw the honour which God put upon him, and the respect paid him by the people, and the greater success attending his preaching, than had followed the preaching of Mr. Edwards immediately before he went to Leicester. I found rest and rejoicing in it, and the sweet language of my soul continually was, "Amen, Lord Jesus! Amen, Lord Jesus!"

At 3 o'clock in the afternoon, a lecture was preached by Mr. Buell. In the latter part of the sermon, one or two appeared much moved, and after the blessing, when the people were going out, several others. To my mind there was the clearest evidence, that God was present in the congregation, on the work of redeeming love; and in the clear view of this, I was all at once filled with such intense admiration of the wonderful condescension and grace of God, in returning again to Northampton, as overwhelmed my soul, and immediately took away my bodily strength. This was accompanied with an earnest longing, that those of us, who were the children of God, might now arise and strive. It appeared to me, that the angels in heaven sung praises, for such wonderful, free and sovereign grace, and my heart was lifted up in the adoration and praise. I continued to have clear views

5

of the future world, of eternal happiness and misery, and my heart full of love to the souls of men. On seeing some, that I found were in a natural condition, I felt a most tender compassion for them; but especially was I, while I remained in the meeting-house, from time to time overcome, and my strength taken away, by the sight of one and another, whom I regarded as the children of God, and who, I had heard were lively and animated in religion. We remained in the meeting-house about three hours, after the public exercises were over. During most of the time, my bodily strength was overcome; and the joy and thankfulness, which were excited in my mind, as I contemplated the great goodness of God, led me to converse with those who were near me, in a very earnest manner.

When I came home, I found Mr. Buell, Mr. Christophers, Mr. Hopkins, Mrs. Eleanor Dwight, the wife of Mr. Joseph Allen, and Mr. Job Strong, at the house.[12] Seeing and conversing with them on the Divine goodness, renewed my former feelings, and filled me with an intense desire that we might all arise, and, with an active, flowing and fervent heart, give glory to God. The intenseness of my feelings again took away my bodily strength. The words of one of Dr. Watts's Hosannas powerfully affected me; and, in the course of the conversation, I uttered them, as the real language of my heart, with great earnestness and emotion.

> "Hosanna to King David's Son,
> "Who reigns on a superior throne," etc.[13]

And while I was uttering the words, my mind was so deeply impressed with the love of Christ, and a sense of his immediate presence, that I could with difficulty refrain from rising from my seat, and leaping for joy. I continued to enjoy this intense, and lively and refreshing sense of Divine things, accompanied with strong emotions, for nearly an hour; after which, I experienced a delightful calm, and peace and rest in God, until I retired for the night; and during the night, both waking and sleeping, I had joyful views of Divine things, and a complacential rest of soul in God. I awoke in the morning of Thursday, January 28th, in the same happy frame of mind, and engaged in the duties of my family with a sweet consciousness, that God was present with me, and with earnest longings of soul for the continuance, and increase, of the blessed fruits of the Holy Spirit in the town.[14] About nine o'clock, these desires became so exceedingly intense, when I saw numbers of the people coming into the house, with an appearance of deep interest in religion, that my bodily strength was much weakened, and it was with difficulty that I could pursue my ordinary avocations. About 11 o'clock, as I accidentally went into the room where Mr. Buell was conversing with some of the people, I heard him say, "O that we, who are the children of God, should be cold and life-less in religion!" and I felt such a sense of the deep ingratitude mani-fested by the children of God, in such coldness and deadness, that my strength was immediately taken away, and I sunk down on the spot. Those who were near raised me, and placed me in a chair; and, from the fulness of my heart, I expressed to them, in a very earnest manner, the deep sense I had of the wonderful grace of Christ towards me, of the assurance I had of his having saved me from hell, of my happiness running parallel with eternity, of the duty of giving up all to God, and of the peace and joy inspired by an entire dependence on his mercy and grace. Mr. Buell then read a melting hymn of Dr. Watts,[15] and the truth and reality of the things mentioned in the hymn, made so strong an impression on my mind, and my soul was drawn so powerfully towards Christ and heaven, that I leaped unconsciously from my chair. I seemed to be drawn upwards, soul and body, from the earth towards heaven; and it appeared to me that I must naturally and necessarily ascend thither. These feelings continued while the hymn was reading, and during the prayer of Mr. Christophers, which followed. After the prayer, Mr. Buell read two other hymns, on the glories of heaven, which moved me so exceedingly, and drew me so strongly heavenward, that it seemed as it were to draw my body upwards, and I felt as if I must necessarily ascend thither. At length my strength failed me, and I sunk down; when they took me up and laid me on the bed, where I lay for a considerable time, faint with joy, while contemplating the glories of the heavenly world. After I had lain a while, I felt more perfectly subdued and weaned from the world, and more fully resigned to God, than I had ever been conscious of before. I felt an entire indifference to the opinions, and representations and conduct of mankind respecting me; and a perfect willingness, that God should employ some other instrument than Mr. Edwards, in advancing the work of grace in Northhampton. I was entirely swallowed up in God, as my only portion, and his honour and glory was the object of my supreme desire and delight. At the same time, I felt a far greater love to the children of God, than ever before. I seemed to love them as my own soul; and when I saw them, my heart went out towards them, with an inexpressible endearedness and sweetness. I beheld them by faith in their risen and glorified state, with spiritual bodies re-fashioned after the image of Christ's glorious body, and arrayed in the beauty of heaven. The time when they would be so, appeared very near, and by faith it seemed as if it were present. This was accompanied with a ravishing sense of the unspeakable joys of the upper world. They appeared to my mind in all their reality and certainty, and as it were in actual and distinct vision; so plain and evident were they to the eye of my faith, I seemed to regard them as begun. These anticipations were renewed over and over, while I lay on the bed, from twelve o'clock till four, being too much exhausted by emotions of joy, to rise and sit up; and during most of the time, my feelings prompted me to converse very earnestly, with one and another of the pious women, who were present, on those spiritual and heavenly objects, of which I had so deep an impression. A little while before I arose, Mr. Buell and the people went to meeting.

I continued in a sweet and lively sense of Divine things, until I retired to rest. That night, which was Thursday night, January 28, was the sweetest night I ever had in my life. I never before, for so long a time together, enjoyed so much of the light, and rest and sweetness of heaven in my soul, but without the least agitation of body during the whole time. The great part of the night I lay awake, sometimes asleep, and sometimes between sleeping and waking. But all night I continued in a constant, clear and lively sense of the heavenly sweetness of Christ's excellent and transcendent love, of his nearness to me, and of my dearness to him; with an inexpressibly sweet calmness of soul in an entire rest in him. I seemed to myself to perceive a glow of divine love come down from the heart of Christ in heaven, into my heart, in a constant stream, like a stream or pencil of sweet light.[16] At the same time, my heart and soul all flowed out in love to Christ; so that there seemed to be a constant flowing and reflowing of heavenly and divine love, from Christ's heart to mine; and I appeared to myself to float or swim, in these bright, sweet beams of the love of Christ, like the motes swimming in the beams of the sun, or the streams of his light which come in at the window. My soul remained in a kind of heavenly elysium. So far as I am capable of making a comparison, I think that what I felt each minute, during the continuance of the whole time, was worth more than all the outward comfort and pleasure, which I had enjoyed in my whole life put together. It was a pure delight, which fed and satisfied the soul. It was pleasure, without the least sting, or any interruption. It was a sweetness, which my soul was lost in. It seemed to be all that my feeble frame could sustain, of that fulness of joy, which is felt by those, who behold the face of Christ, and share his love in the heavenly world. There was but little difference, whether I was asleep or awake, so deep was the impression made on my soul; but if

there was any difference, the sweetness was greatest and most uninter-
rupted, while I was asleep.

As I awoke early the next morning, which was Friday, I was led to
think of Mr. Williams of Hadley preaching that day in the town, as had
been appointed; and to examine my heart, whether I was willing that he,
who was a neighbouring minister, should be extraordinarily blessed, and
made a greater instrument of good in the town, than Mr. Edwards; and
was enabled to say, with respect to that matter, "Amen, Lord Jesus!" and
to be entirely willing, if God pleased, that he should be the instrument of
converting every soul in the town. My soul acquiesced fully in the will of
God, as to the will of God, as to the instrument, if his work of renewing
grace did but go on.

This lively sense of the beauty and excellency of divine things, continued during the morning, accompanied with peculiar sweetness and
delight. To my own imagination, my soul seemed to be gone out of me
to God and Christ in heaven, and to have very little relation to my body.
God and Christ were so present to me, and so near me, that I seemed
removed from myself. The spiritual beauty of the Father and the Saviour,
seemed to engross my whole mind; and it was the instinctive feeling of
my heart, "Thou art; and there is none beside thee."[17] I never felt such an
entire emptiness of self-love, or any regard to any private, selfish interest
of my own. It seemed to me, that I had entirely done with myself. I felt
that the opinions of the world concerning me were nothing, and that I
had no more to do with any outward interest of my own, than with that
of a person whom I never saw. The glory of God seemed to be all, and in
all, and to swallow up every wish and desire of my heart.

Mr. Sheldon came into the house about 10 o'clock, and said to me as
he came in, "The Sun of righteousness arose on my soul this morning,
before day;" upon which I said to him in reply, "That Sun has not set upon
my soul all this night; I have dwelt on high in the heavenly mansions; the
light of divine love has surrounded me; my soul has been lost in God, and
has almost left the body."[18] This conversation only served to give me a still
livelier sense of the reality and excellence of divine things, and that to such
a degree, as again to take away my strength, and occasion great agitation of
body. So strong were my feelings, I could not refrain from conversing with
those around me, in a very earnest manner, for about a quarter of an hour,
on the infinite riches of divine love in the work of salvation: when, my
strength entirely failing, my flesh grew very cold, and they carried me and
set me by the fire. As I sat there, I had a most affecting sense of the mighty

power of Christ, which had been exerted in what he had done for my soul, and in sustaining and keeping down the native corruptions of my heart, and of the glorious and wonderful grace of God in causing the ark to return to Northampton. So intense were my feelings, when speaking of these things, that I could not forbear rising up and leaping with joy and exultation. I felt at the same time an exceedingly strong and tender affection for the children of God, and realized, in a manner exceedingly sweet and ravishing, the meaning of Christ's prayer, in John 17:21, *"That they all may be one, as thou Father art in me, and I in thee, that they also may be one in us."* This union appeared to me an inconceivable, excellent and sweet oneness; and at the same time I felt that oneness in my soul, with the children of God who were present. Mr. Christophers then read the hymn out of the Penitential Cries, beginning with

> "My soul doth magnify the Lord,
> "My spirit doth rejoice;"

The whole hymn was deeply affecting to my feelings: but when these words were read,

> "My sighs at length are turn'd to songs,
> "The Comforter is come:"—[19]

So conscious was I of the joyful presence of the holy Spirit, I could scarcely refrain from leaping with transports of joy. This happy frame of mind continued until two o'clock, when Mr. Williams came in, and we soon went to meeting. He preached on the subject of the assurance of faith. The whole sermon was affecting to me, but especially when he came to show the way in which assurance was obtained, and to point out its happy fruits. When I heard him say that *those, who have assurance, have a foretaste of heavenly glory,* I knew the truth of it from what I then felt: I knew that I then tasted the clusters of the heavenly Canaan: My soul was filled and overwhelmed with light, and love, and joy in the Holy Ghost, and seemed just ready to go away from the body. I could scarcely refrain from expressing my joy aloud, in the midst of the service. I had in the mean time, an overwhelming sense of the glory of God, as the Great Eternal All, and of the happiness of having my own will entirely subdued to his will. I knew that the foretaste of glory, which I then had in my soul, came from him, that I certainly should go to him, and should, as it were, drop into the Divine Being, and be swallowed up in God.

After meeting was done, the congregation waited while Mr. Buell went home, to prepare to give them a Lecture. It was almost dark before he came, and, in the mean time, I conversed in a very earnest and joyful manner, with those who were with me in the pew. My mind dwelt on the thought, that the Lord God Omnipotent reigneth, and it appeared to me that he was going to set up a Reign of Love on the earth, and that heaven and earth were, as it were, coming together; which so exceedingly moved me that I could not forbear expressing aloud, to those near me, my exultation of soul. This subsided into a heavenly calm, and a rest of soul in God, which was even sweeter than what preceded it. Afterwards, Mr. Buell came and preached; and the same happy frame of mind continued during the evening, and night, and the next day. In the forenoon, I was thinking of the manner in which the children of God had been treated in the world—particularly of their being shut up in prison—and the folly of such attempts to make them miserable, seemed to surprise me. It appeared astonishing, that men should think, by this means, to injure those who had such a kingdom within them. Towards night, being informed that Mrs. P— had expressed her fears least I should die before Mr. Edwards' return, and he should think the people had killed his wife;[20] I told those who were present, that I chose to die in the way that was most agreeable to God's will, and that I should be willing to die in darkness and horror, if it was most for the glory of God.

In the evening, I read those chapters in John, which contain Christ's dying discourse with his disciples, and his prayer with them.[21] After I had done reading, and was in my retirement, a little before bed-time, thinking on what I had read, my soul was so filled with love to Christ, and love to his people, that I fainted under the intenseness of the feeling. I felt, while reading, a delightful acquiescence in the petition to the Father—"I *pray not that thou shouldst take them out of the world, but that thou shouldst keep them from the evil.*" Though it seemed to me infinitely better to die to go to Christ, yet I felt an entire willingness to continue in this world so long as God pleased, to do and suffer what he would have me.

After retiring to rest and sleeping a little while, I awoke and had a very lively consciousness of God's being near me. I had an idea of a shining way, or path of light, between heaven and my soul, somewhat as on Thursday night, except that God seemed nearer to me, and as it were close by, and the way seemed more open, and the communication more immediate and more free. I lay awake most of the night, with a constant delightful sense of God's great love and infinite condescension, and with a

continual view of God as *near*, and as *my God*. My soul remained, as on
Thursday night, in a kind of heavenly elysium. Whether waking or sleeping, there was no interruption, throughout the night, to the views of my
soul, to its heavenly light, and divine, inexpressible sweetness. It was
without any agitation or motion of the body. I was led to reflect on God's
mercy to me, in giving me, for many years, a willingness to die; and after
that, for more than two years past, in making me willing to live, that I
might do and suffer whatever he called me to here; whereas, before that,
I often used to feel impatient at the thought of living. This then appeared
to me, as it had often done before, what gave me much the greatest sense
of thankfulness to God. I also thought how God had graciously given me,
for a great while, an entire resignation to his will, with respect to the kind
and manner of death that I should die; having been made willing to die
on the rack, or at the stake, or any other tormenting death, and, if it were
God's will, to die in darkness: and how I had that day been made very sensible and fully willing, if it was God's pleasure and for his glory, to die in
horror. But now it occurred to me, that when I had thus been made willing to live, and to be kept on this dark abode, I used to think of living no
longer than to the ordinary age of man. Upon this I was led to ask myself,
Whether I was not willing to be kept out of heaven even longer; and my
whole heart seemed immediately to reply, "Yes, a thousand years, if it be
God's will, and for his honour and glory:" and then my heart, in the language of resignation, went further, and with great alacrity and sweetness,
to answer as it were over and over again, "Yes, and live a thousand years
in horror, if it be most for the glory of God: yea, I am willing to live a
thousand years an hell upon earth, if it be most for the honour of God."
But then I considered with myself, What this would be, to live an hell
upon earth, for so long a time; and I thought of the torment of my body
being so great, awful and overwhelming, that none could bear to live in
the country where the spectacle was seen, and of the torment and horror
of my mind being vastly greater than the torment of my body; and it
seemed to me that I found a perfect willingness, and sweet quietness and
alacrity of soul, in consenting that it should be so, if it were most for the
glory of God; so that there was no hesitation, doubt or darkness in my
mind, attending the thoughts of it, but my resignation seemed to be clear,
like a light that shone through my soul. I continued saying, "Amen, Lord
Jesus! Amen, Lord Jesus! glorify thyself in me, in my body and my
soul,"—with a calm and sweetness of soul, which banished all reluctance.
The glory of God seemed to overcome me and swallow me up, and every

conceivable suffering, and every thing that was terrible to my nature, seemed to shrink to nothing before it. This resignation continued in its clearness and brightness the rest of the night, and all the next day, and the night following, and on Monday in the forenoon, without interruption or abatement. All this while, whenever I thought of it, the language of my soul was, with the greatest fullness and alacrity, "Amen, Lord Jesus! Amen, Lord Jesus!" In the afternoon of Monday, it was not quite so perceptible and lively, but my mind remained so much in a similar frame, for more than a week, that I could never think of it without an inexpressible sweetness in my soul.

After I had felt this resignation on Saturday night, for some time as I lay in bed, I felt such a disposition to rejoice in God, that I wished to have the world join me in praising him; and was ready to wonder how the world of mankind could lie and sleep, when there was such a God to praise, and rejoice in, and could scarcely forbear calling out to those who were asleep in the house, to arise, and rejoice, and praise God. When I arose on the morning of the Sabbath, I felt a love to all mankind, wholly peculiar in its strength and sweetness, far beyond all that I had ever felt before. The power of that love seemed to be inexpressible. I thought, if I were surrounded by enemies, who were venting their malice and cruelty upon me, in tormenting me, it would still be impossible that I should cherish any feelings towards them but those of love, and pity and ardent desires for their happiness. At the same time I thought, if I were cast off by my nearest and dearest friends, and if the feelings and conduct of my husband were to be changed from tenderness and affection, to extreme hatred and cruelty, and that every day, I could so rest in God, that it would not touch my heart, or diminish my happiness. I could still go on with alacrity in the performance of every act of duty, and my happiness remain undiminished and entire.

I never before felt so far from a disposition to judge and censure others, with respect to the state of their hearts, their sincerity, or their attainments in holiness, as I did that morning. To do this, seemed abhorrent to every feeling of my heart. I realized also, in an unusual and very lively manner, how great a part of christianity lies in the performance of our social and relative duties to one another. The same lively and joyful sense of spiritual and divine things continued throughout the day—a sweet love to God and all mankind, and such an entire rest of soul in God, that it seemed as if nothing that could be said of me, or done to me, could touch my heart, or disturb my enjoyment. The road between heaven and my soul seemed open and wide, all the day long; and the consciousness I had of the reality and excellence of heavenly things was so clear, and the affections they excited so intense, that it overcame my strength, and kept my body weak and faint, the great part of the day, so that I could not stand or go without help. The night also was comforting and refreshing.

This delightful frame of mind was continued on Monday. About noon, one of the neigbours, who was conversing with me, expressed himself thus, "One smile from Christ is worth a thousand million pounds," and the words affected me exceedingly, and in a manner which I cannot express. I had a strong sense of the infinite worth of Christ's approbation and love, and at the same time of the grossness of the comparison; and it only astonished me, that any one could compare a smile of Christ to any earthly treasure. —Towards night, I had a deep sense of the awful greatness of God, and felt with what humility and reverence we ought to behave ourselves before him. Just then Mr. W— came in, and spoke with a somewhat light, smiling air, of the flourishing state of religion in the town; which I could scarcely bear to see. It seemed to me, that we ought greatly to revere the presence of God, and to behave ourselves with the utmost solemnity and humility, when so great and holy a God was so remarkably present, and to rejoice before him with trembling. —In the evening, these words, in the Penitential Cries, —"THE COMFORTER IS COME!"—were accompanied to my soul with such conscious certainty, and such intense joy, that immediately it took away my strength, and I was falling to the floor; when some of those who were near me caught me and held me up.[22] And when I repeated the words to the by-standers, the strength of my feelings was increased. The name— "THE COMFORTER"—seemed to denote that the Holy Spirit was the only and infinite Fountain of comfort and joy, and this seemed real and certain to my mind. These words— "THE COMFORTER"— seemed as it were immensely great, enough to fill heaven and earth.

On Tuesday after dinner, Mr. Buell, as he sat at table, began to discourse about the glories of the upper world; which greatly affected me, so as to take away my strength. The views and feelings of the preceding evening, respecting the Great Comforter, were renewed in the most lively and joyful manner; so that my limbs grew cold, and I continued to a considerable degree overcome for about an hour, earnestly expressing to those around me, my deep and joyful sense of the presence and divine excellence of the Comforter, and of the glories of heaven.

It was either on Tuesday, or Wednesday, that Mr. W— came to the house, and informed what account Mr. Lyman, who was just then come from Leicester, on his way from Boston, gave of Mr. Edwards' success, in making peace and promoting religion at Leicester.[23] The intelligence inspired me with such an admiring sense of the great goodness of God, in using Mr. Edwards as the instrument of doing good, and promoting the work of salvation, that it immediately overcame me, and took away my strength, so that I could no longer stand on my feet. On Wednesday night, Mr. Clark, coming in with Mr. Buell and some of the people, asked me how I felt.[24] I told him that I did not feel at all times alike, but this I thought I could say, that I had given up all to God, and there is nothing like it, nothing like giving up all to him, esteeming all to be his, and resigning all at his call. I told him that, many a time within a twelve-month, I had asked myself when I lay down, How should I feel, if our house and all our property in it should be burnt up, and we should that night be turned out naked; whether I could cheerfully resign all to God; and whether I so saw that all was his, that I could fully consent to his will, in being deprived of it? and that I found, so far as I could judge, an entire resignation to his will, and felt that, if he should thus strip me of every thing, I had nothing to say, but should, I thought, have an entire calm and rest in God, for it was his own, and not mine. After this, Mr. Phelps gave us an account of his own feelings, during a journey from which he had just returned; and then Mr. Pomeroy broke forth in the language of joy, and thankfulness and praise, and continued speaking to us nearly an hour, leading us all the time to rejoice in the visible presence of God, and to adore his infinite goodness and condescension.[25] He concluded by saying, "I would say more, if I could; but words were not made to express these things." This reminded me of the words of Mrs. Rowe:

> "More I would speak, but all my words are faint:
> "Celestial Love, what eloquence can paint?
> "No more, by mortal words, can be expressed;
> "But vast Eternity shall tell the rest;"[26]

and my former impressions of heavenly and divine things were renewed with so much power, and life and joy, that my strength all failed me, and I remained for some time faint and exhausted. After the people had retired, I had a still more lively and joyful sense of the goodness and all-sufficiency of God, of the pleasure of loving him, and of being alive and active in his service, so that, I could not sit still, but walked the room for some time, in a kind of transport. The contemplation was so refreshing and delightful, so much like a heavenly feast within the soul, that I felt an absolute indifference as to any external circumstances; and, according to my best remembrance, this enlivening of my spirit continued so, that I slept but little that night.

The next day, being Thursday, between ten and eleven o'clock, and a room full of people being collected, I heard two persons give a minute account of the enlivening and joyful influences of the Holy Spirit on their own hearts. It was sweet to me, to see others before me in their divine attainments, and to follow after them to heaven. I thought I should rejoice to follow the negro servants in the town to heaven. While I was thus listening, the consideration of the blessed appearances there were of God's being there with us, affected me so powerfully, that the joy and transport of the preceding night were again renewed. After this, they sang an hymn, which greatly moved me, especially the latter part of it, which speaks of the ungratefulness of not having the praises of Christ always on our tongues. Those last words of the hymn seemed to fasten on my mind, and I repeated them over, I felt such intense love to Christ, and so much delight in praising him, that I could hardly forbear leaping from my chair, and singing aloud for joy and exultation. I continued thus extraordinarily moved until about one o'clock, when the people went away."

"My Chosen and only Sure Friend"

The Spiritual Narrative of Sarah Prince Gill

[Undated]

In the y[ear] 1743 reading Mr White *On the Power of Godliness,* I was convinced that it is my duty to comit to writing My Experiences;[1] [I] hope it will be a means of keeping alive the work[ings] of Grace in me—And excite me to be maki[ng] Progress in Religion—Accordingly I set about it in the Fear of God who searches the Heart and trieth the Ruins—And beggin[g] the assistances of his Holy Spirit to bring all thing[s] to My Remembrance.

Miss Gill

I was born July 16, 1728, and was solemnly Devoted to the Blessed God in Baptism—Was religiously Educated [and] had the Advantage of Frequent hearing the Word Preached and other Publick means of Grace— And God was Pleased from his meer Sovereign Pleasure to Grant me the common Restraints of his Grace. And at times some awakenings of Conscience—all which Favor call'd aloud for the most gratefull Returns—But alass, I Quenched the Motions of His spirit—Made the Pleasing my Self the End of all my Designs and Actions. Liv'd in Ignorance of and Estrangement from the blessed God, took the World for my Portion, and for the most Part liv'd securely 'Tho I had something of tenderness of conscience. And was sometimes resolved to Practice secret Prayer, etc. but cou'd not hold it Long—And thus I liv'd the 1st *Twelve Years* of my Life in a Great Measure tho'tless of God and Eternity. O, what wonder it is that God did not cut me down as a Cumberer of his Ground![2]—When Mr Whitefield came to Boston [in] 1740 I was something affected with his Ministry[3]—But I believe only my Passions were moved—Or if at any time his Sermon came close to me, I Put it off to a more Convenient Season— However, I began a constant course of secret Prayer and reading often Pious books—and Tho't I was converted because I took some Delight in Duty—When Mr Tennent came, Multitudes were awakened to a sence of their Deplorable state while out of Christ, and not a few we have reason to hope were savingly bro't home to God thro' Christ.[4] This something alarmed me [and] some of my Acquaintance [who] were tho'tfull about their souls, and we used to meet to Pray and confer about spiritual things—About this time, a sermon of Mr Coopers was attended with impressions on my conscience from Eph. 1:19.[5] O, the many Powerfull Discourses I heard that Winter and yet how little affected? For my convictions were not thoro'—'till November 17, 1741, when hearing a sermon of Mr Wheelocks from Hos. 13:13—I was convinced that I was in a Dredfull state under the Wrath and curse of God [and] Exposed to the Execution of it.[6] Every moment I saw that I had bro't my Misery upon My self and the Distress I was in, yet I tho't I was not distressed Enough. I heard him Preach a solemn sermon from Ezek. 22:14; then the Terrors of God were put in array against me—I saw My Enmity to God as I never did before; I was afraid to go to sleep lest I shou'd awake in [. . .] I saw it was my Duty to believe in Christ, but I found I cou'd not do it more than Create a World. Sometimes I Grew Pretty Easy, and then I was afraid if I lost convictions now, they wou'd never return. I had a veiw of the corruption of my Heart—O, I tho't it was like a heap of Rubbish that when it was stirred up, all manner of abominations appeared in it—Thus I went on the Winter of 41, 2. In April 1742, I heard a sermon from Sol Song 11[7]—Wherein the manner of the Believer Espous'd to Christ was described that the soul is willing to Quit all Pretences to salvation upon any other [. . .] but the merits of Christ and so sets the Crown on his head by yeilding to this method of salvation and Giving the Glory of its salvation to him alone which Temper of Soul I thought I found in my self—I tho't I saw the Excellency of Christ and had my soul fill'd with Love to Him—I tho't I found an immediate alteration in my self, Particularly Peace and serenity of soul and an Earnest desire to glorify God. Longings for the Salvation of Others—I wanted all to tast[e] and see that God is Good. Now the tho'ts of Christ were Precious to me, And discourse about any other object a burden.[8] Sometimes I cou'd hardly believe, for I [. . .] and wondered. I heard a sermon from Ps. 45:5, and I tho't I found the marks of those that fall down under Christ upon my heart—As also from 1 John 1:7 And had reason to think I had Experienced communion with God—The ordinances of God were more Precious, and I could not be contented with out the Presence of Christ in them—But O, how did my Corruptions mix in with Grace, Especially Pride.[9] War against a particular corruption, notice well John 10:4, 5 Matt. 6:24, Prov. 24:9, John 5:21, etc.[10] I was often Lifted up in my own apprehensions above others—O, what a dishonour it was to God—And what a wonder it was that he did not leave me to the buffetings of Satan and vanity of my heart. But he knew my Ignorance and weakness and pitied me. And I trust has *gradually enlightened me in the Knowledge of his Will and Way* and has (in some measure) taught me to distinguish between the workin[g]s of Imagination and Grace. I think I had frequent returns of Darkness as to my state—but often was made to rejoice in the ways of God. And one Error that I went into was Judging of my Experiences and those of others— Whereas the word of God is the only standard, this made me walk very uncomfortably,[11] and I particularly remember the many persons whom I look'd upon to be Experienced Christians Invited (that there must be a word of Promise bore in on the soul at the time of Conversion) and I not having any, it greatly Perplex'd me—But not writing down my Experiences, I can't tell how I was from Day to Day—Only in the General that I indulged a careless, sloth-full Frame and fell into Great Deadness and so remained until October: when hearing a sermon from Ps. 3:7, 8. Then I humbly hope God satisfied me with the rulings of his house and made me want of the River of his Pleasure—I was helped renewedly to embrace the Lord Jesus in all his offices—That Night I was greatly affected with the Love of God to me, an ungratefull wretch; I saw I had abused his Grace, and yet he manifested himself to me as he does not to the World. And I thought I had Communion with God—The next Sabbath I heard Dear Mr Edwards from John 12:32.[12] I trust I had the Presence of Christ with me; and by the Marks laid down, I concluded I had been Drawn to Christ.[13] At Noon I was left to tell a Lie—But my Conscience smote me and I was in great distress. Mr *Cooper* was led in his Prayer to Set forth sin in its true coulours. I hearing how vile our hearts are from whence Proceed all actual sins, also to the ungratefullness of sin, etc.; but all at once He broke out into the Expressions: "Lord, we repair to the blood of Christ which is a fountain opened to cleanse as from all Sin." I was inabled to go to Christ for Pardon and cleansing and was assured that he had forgiven me. I felt Pretty comfortable the day after particularly. One Eve when Mr Edwards Preached on the Humiliation and sufferings of the Son of God from Heb. 5:7, he was much assisted in the discourse, and I trust the truths delivered were [ac]companied with divine Power on my heart— I mourned for sin as the worst Evil—I Loathed and abhorred My self as a Monster of Ingratitude; and although I thought God had forgiven me and Christ had died for me having bore my Sins in his own body on the tree that I might live forever, yet I cou'd not forgive My self. I came home bitterly bewailing my *sinfull heart*, condemning My self, and

Repenting in Dust and Ashes. I had a Lively View of the sufferings of Christ for sin and for My sins in Particular and I [. . .] I had that Godly Sorrow which worketh penitence and those other fruits mentioned in 2 Cor. 7:2—O, how hatefull sin appears when by Faith we see it Represented in the Sufferings and Death of the dear Redeemer—I don't remember the frame of my Mind for some time after this—In the Winter following, vis 42/3, I fell into decay, became Carnal and Worldly, and gave a dredfull scope to vain Imaginations which caused me to doubt of My state hereby (vis, my earthly temper). I lost the Evidence of *Sanctification*; and if I looked back on what I had Experienced, I feared it was only the Common Work of the spirit of God and My own Imagination; for the tree is to be Judged by the Fruit[14]—And here I seem'd to Rest—Sometimes I was very uneasy and yet was unwilling to give up what hope I had of (my good state). I almost lost a relish for Spiritual Things, [and] holy Conversation was not so aggreable as it used to be—I was much under a spirit of [B]ondage, was Exceedingly Terrefied at Thunder and Lightning, [and] was afraid of Death[15]—I believe never a child of God wandred so far from as I did then—And thus I continued the bigest Part of the following summer—Tho' I was sensible, I was in a Miserable [ca]se Inddeed and uttered My Complaints before God in the Language of Job: "O, that it was with me as in months past," etc.[16]—I believe God suffered it thus to be for wise and holy Ends, to humble me for the Pride of My heart, to teach me to depend on him only, and not to rest on any Experiences or Attainments of my own, to Excite me to a Strict watch over my [hea]rt and Life, and to Labour after greater Nearness [to] Him—O Lord, humble me to the Dust for this dredfull temper whereby I have dishonored Thee [and] make me more carefull for the future—Help me to shun Even the Appearance of Evil, and as I have dishonored thee by a Worldly Frame, So help me to honour thee by a heavenly temper. In the Latter End of Sumer 1743, I came to be more serious and in August went to [. . .] to a Lecture—But was so vain and airy that My Conscience Flew in my Face for pretending to Go to worship God—And yet Indulging so much Levity and we all tho't we had better have staid at home—However, we went into meeting; Mr T[. . .]t[17] was preaching from Eph. 5:1—["]Be yee followers of God as dear children." At first I was much chagrin'd because the *Minister* I came to hear was not Preaching, he being the Person I thought God made an Instrument of My Conversion. I had a Peculiar Value for his Preaching. I mark this because it renders the following Experience more astonishing, that God shou'd appear for me and manifest his Love to me at the time I was quarreling with his Providence and Ordinance—It is a display of the sovereignty of Grace which superabounds to the vilest of sinners. After Mr T[. . .] Sermon [. . .], another Minister Preached from Cor. 2:6 from which He showed the just Nature of Faith and the Manner of its operations in the First Closure with Christ[18] and then what an "answerable walk" is. And under the First, I was Led to reflect [my] own experiences and to Compare them with the laws laid down—The Manner of my First closing with the Lord Jesus was distinctly brought to My remembrance— And I Judged that I had Experienced a true Conversion—Under the Second, I compared my Walk and O, how unanswerable! How Unholy! What little progress in grace! How unproffitable! How little have I done for God—I was ashamed and even confounded—I was astonished at the sovereign Grace of God, and at my own vile Ingratitude; it was (I saw) beyound the force of Words to Express my [b]aseness—I mourned for my contrariety to God [and] for My careless walk before him—for the dishonour I had done him—I magnified and praised him for his Great Grace to me in manifesting himself to me as he does not to the World and saw it must all proceed from his Sovereign Grace—He will have mercy on whom he will have Mercy!—I enjoyed much of Divine Presence in a Journey I took to Leicester, and in October I was quickned by the Powerfull preaching of Mr Owen[19]—O, how did my soul thirst after Holiness; as the heart panteth after the water brooks, so did my soul after perfect purity.[20] All sin, even the most beloved, was hatefull to me. I loved God because he is Holy and I lov'd Holiness. Wherever it appeared, my soul was drawn to those that I thought bore the Image of God, Especially if the[y] appeared Meek and Humble. I longed to be meek and Lowly in heart and to be possessed of a Christ like temper [and] [exa]amined My self as to the reasons of My hope And I found them to be these, vis

1. Because I have fled for Refuge to the hope set before me in the Gosple.

2. Because I find a hatred of all sin because it is a Dishonour to God.

3. I find an ardent desire and love to Holiness seeing an Infinite Beauty in it.

4. I desire to be perfectly free from all Sin, and to do and suffer what ever God would have me and to be entirely ruled and led by him, to have My Will entirely Subjected to him in all things, making no reservation.

OCTOBER 28, 1743
Friday

I hope I was enabled to give up My self to God, to be disposed of as he saw fit and to acquiesce in his Will. As I was pondering on My own Departour out of the world, I was made willing God shou'd order it just as he pleased and if his Glory shou'd be manifested by My suffering (in that important Period), doubts, and distress about my state, I was willing he shou'd take me out of the World in those Uncomfortable cases—O, that My Will may be always swallowed up in his Will. Amen.

Eve
As I was thinking on the Unkindness of one, I was too much ruffled and dejected about it when those Words Isa. 49:15–16 Came to My Mind with a Sweet Power. I Was assured that my heavenly Father wou'd not forget me, for I cou'd rest upon his Word who is true and Faithfull [and] who can never forget his people. Grant, O Lord, that I may never Question thy Faithfullness.

NOVEMBER 4, 1743
Friday

I have for some days past been assaulted with temptation to Disbelieve the Divinity of Christ! O, what a Subtle, Crafty Enemy we have to encounter![21] Satan knows if he can bring us to reject this Grand Article of our Faith, all the rest will be of no Effect. For if Christ is not the Mighty God as well as the Prince of Peace, he is not a Saviour sufficient to trust the weighty concerns of immortal spirits with: But blessed be the Captain of our Salvation who is stronger than the strong man armed.[22] I hope he this day Granted me a farther deliverance from the Lion of hell;[23] for while I was waiting on God in the use of his apointed means and was reading the first chapter of St. Johns Gosple, I hope I beheld in this Glass the Divine Glory of the Lord Jesus and by the teaching of his spirit was led to See that Christ was God, Co-equal with the father, the same in substance, equal in Power and equal in Glory, that he was from Eternity and no created being—I have now found it Good to wait on God—I desire to Continue in this Way of seeking (in the use of means) the further Instructions of his spirit that I may be led in to all the Truths he has revealed and that he wou'd enable me to embrace them—For I feel my Impotence! And I see my Ignorance.

Bless the Lord, O my soul, for this instance of his kindness and live to the Praise of his Grace.

NOVEMBER 1743

I feel such a war in me, flesh Lusting against spirit, and spirit striving against Flesh, that I often breath[e] out my complaints and desires in Dr Watts words:

> I'm like a helpless Captive sold
> Under the power of sin
> I cannot do the good I wou'd
> Nor keep my Conscience clean
> My God I cry with ev'ry breath
> For thy kind power to save
> So break the Yoke of Sin and death
> And thus redeem the slave[24]

DECEMBER 11, 1743
Sunday

Was fill'd with earnest desires after Christ all day; as the hart panteth after the water brooks, so did My soul for the living Water. I was restless, and felt I cou'd not be satisfied with out him—I was willing (I thought) to part with all for him and thought I wou'd relinquish a Thousand Worlds if I had them for this pearl of Price[25]—When I went to Meeting in the after noon to seek him whom my soul desired, there was a Bill put up for the rev'd Mr *Cooper* [who is] very Dangerously Ill. My heart was immediatly drawn out in Love to this Excellent servant of Christ—I was exceedingly distressed with the apprehension of Loosing him; and I repeatedly Importuned for his recovery. Anon, which this Thought came in to my Mind: *Will you have Christ or Mr Cooper?* And My Heart answered, I'll part with Mr Cooper for Christ! But soon after, my Tho'ts returned to Mr Cooper, and all the while Mr Cooper was sick and for sometime after his Death, I had such a sence of the hand of God, his Angry Hand in it in removing such a sound and able Divine, so Resolute and Zealous, so active and vigilant, so prudent, so pious, so Experienced, and beloved, and so Usefull a Minister in the midst of his Days. When we wanted him so much and that in such a sudden [and] an awfull Manner, that I cou'd

23

think hardly on any thing Else—O, that God wou'd pardon me for what was amiss herein for the sake of Christ, Amen.

FEBRUARY 15, 1744
Thursday

I have this day heard an Excellent sermon from Rom. 7:22. But O, this Body of Sin and Death which cleaves to me and separates me from God [and] which makes him hide his Lovely Face and render me so unlike him. O, wretched one that I am! How full of sin? It creeps in to My Frames before I am aware;[26] It mingles with every tho't and with every duty, and I cannot See thro' the disguise nor find it half out—I find a Law in my members warring against the Law in My mind, and it brings me into Captivity that when I wou'd do good, evil is present with me—I want to have all sin rooted out of me—I want to be Conformed to the Image of Christ, to Die Daily to sin, and live to Righteousness—to be crucifying my old Man, to Pluck out my beloved lust, [and] to have my Conscience purged from dead works to Serve the Living God. And inasmuch as Perfection is not attainable in this Life, I long for that blessed Time when I shall be taken out of it and be made perfect in holiness in the full, enjoying of God thro' Eternity.

MARCH 24, 1744
Saturday Eve

I would set My self in the presence of *God* to Examine with care and Deliveration [Deliberation?] My self, whether I am the Subject of a Work of *Conviction, Convertion,* [and] *Sanctification,* 1st Original Sin, actual sin, Indwelling sin, and think I find as follows: I see it was just in God to make a Covenant with Adam as our head and Representative [and] that If he continued to walk according to the Precepts of that covenant, he and his posterity shou'd live; otherwise, they shou'd die. I see also that is was Just in God to leave *Adam* the Freedom of his own Will.

And as he fell, so I see it to be Just in God to impute his sin to him and his posterity.

And as all mankind are born sinners, Guilty, and polluted and have their natures totally depraved thro' the first apostacy, so they soon discover this in the first scenes of Life in Pride, Envy, Malice, revenge, self will, self Love, quarrelling, Anger, Lying, Loveing, Play, and other things above God, etc..

And as we grow in years, we grow more averse to God and Holiness and more prone to sin; yea, we fill up our Lives with sin—And besides all these outward and visible sins, their are inumerable sins of a secret Nature which shew that our Hearts and consciences are defiled—And is it not Just in God who is a Being of Infinite Holiness that cannot bear with sin, who has an intire unalterable right to the obediance of all his Creatures, who spared not the Angels, these higher and more noble spirits but doom'd them all to Hell, their to bear his Wrath with out a reprieve for ever, I say, Is it not Just in God to punish such Sinfull worms of the dust as we are that are continually rising up in rebellion against such a Great, Glorious, and Lovely being, to punish us in hell with out the Least hope of Mercy forever? Yes, Yes, Yes, I think I can say (to God alone be the Glory) I have been experimentally convinced of these things; that I have been brought to see in some measure the Plague of my own heart and the vileness of my Life, and to see that it was Just in God to condemn me to Eternal Missery.

(2)
As to Convertion—I hope I have thro' the all conquering Power of Christ and the exceeding Riches and freeness of his Grace been made willing to accept of him as the Prophet, Priest, and King of his salvation and Devote and Give up My self to him to be Ruled, Governed, and Saved by him and have a temper of mind to ascribe the Whole Glory of my salvation to Him.

(3)
As to Sanctification. I hope the work of sanctification is carried on in some measure in me—that I hate all Sin, because it is contrary to God—that I mourn the Remainder of Sin in me and beg to be purged more from it and to be made more holy—that I desire to have my will brought into an intire Subjection to the will of God—to resign to him in those things that are most adverse to my carnal eye and pleasure. I desire (if my heart does not decieve me) to obey all his commands and to serve him wholly.

July 21, 1744
Saturday

It has pleased God to exercise me with a sore trial for these 7 weeks past in the grievous *sickness* and *Death* of My dear and Eldest *sister* who slept in Jesus about seven o'clock last night.[27]

She was a very pleasant and profitable companion—Had a lively, ingenious turn of tho't—a portion of a solid Judgement—a quick apprehension of admirable Prudence. Of a pleasant, free, [and] humble Temper, which was much improved by the Grace of God, evidently governing her of a very tender conscience, a very sincere and faithfull friend to me on all accounts, more especially in those of the greatest importance—In the former part of her sickness, I was not duly concerned for her but felt stupid—The Last 3 weeks I was convinced that she was in great danger; then I felt concerned and the more as she was in great darkness and distress of soul apprehending her self to be a stranger to the saving work of the Spirit of God. When we found she was evidently struck with death, she was in extream agonies of soul. It was eno' to melt the hardest heart to see her—I cou'd not bear the chamber, but with my Brother retired to another where we both walk'd and cryed in the distress of our souls for so dear and so valuable a sister—Our Moans might have been heard far off—My dear sister Mercy (who had so great a degree of firmness as to stay with My dear Debby) came to us and begged we wou'd compose our selves, for said she "What a dishonour is it to Religion; and what will its enemies say; will they not reproach the ways of God, etc.?"—I replyed with earnestness, "'Tis for her soul which is worth 10,000 worlds and I can't bear it shou'd go out of the world in uncertainties, upon which she left us."[28] My Brother imediately replyed, "Do you doubt of her state? I have no doubt but she will be happy, tho' 'tis grievous to see her in this darkness." I answered him, "What are your reasons for being so afraid of the goodness of her state?" (For tho' I had entertained the same opinion of her, yet now I saw the importance and worth of her soul. I tho't no evidence wou'd content me unless she had assurance also.) But before he cou'd reply to me, My dear sister M[ercy] returned and with the tears trickling down her said, "Come into the chamber, for I can't express My Joy." We hasted to the bed side of our dying sister and foun'd that every clou'd was scattered and [that] God had lifted up the light of his Countenance on her.[29] The particular Circumstances of that ever memorable Scene are related in my Fathers Sermon on the Occasion.[30] How was the Scene altered in a moment when a ray of divine light broke in upon her, and her mouth was opened to declare the wonder of divine power and Grace. The Chamber which a minute before was full of distress and anguish now fill'd with Joy, Praise, Love, and Admiration; we to whom she was dearest were the most willing to part with her—For my part, I was intirely willing, I tho't, were it left to my option whether she shou'd stay here and commit more Sin or to now to be made perfectly Holy and so perfectly Happy, I shou'd rather chuse the Latter—And besides, I felt the Love of Christ powerfully constraining me to resign her to death now because he apointed her to it now—I then knew what it was to rejoice in tribulation—and saw the divine reality of our holy religion prov'd by an irresistible demonstration—I felt in this desireable temper for many hours—But alass! The next day I began to reflect on my great loss with much anxiety and disatisfaction—O, I found it beyond the power of Man to bear up under such a greivous stroke—May I follow my dear deceased sister wherein she followed Christ! May I imatate her in Humility, Mortification, self denial, Patience, condescention, etc.. May I profit by her death, heer the call of God in it, [and] prepare for my own end. May my last Moments be my best. Amen, Lord Jesus, Amen.

OCTOBER 7, 1744
Sunday P.M. confin'd

How distinguishing is the goodness of God to me since my being taken sick to this time about 2 months?—He has dealt exceeding gentle with me: has preserved my Life and is reviving me when he has taken away my Dear Sister Debby, who brought more glory to him than ever I have done—I am a barren Fig tree; it wou'd be just in God to cut me down as a cumberer of his Ground, but he deals not with me according to my sins; but as the heavens are high above the earth, so are his Thoughts; his Ways of mercy [are] above my Shallow conceptions.

O Lord! Sanctify mercies and afflictions; may both work my Spiritual Good. Help me to bring Glory to Thee [and] To live answerable to the mercies I receive from Thee. Amen.

NOVEMBER 18, 1744
Sunday

Still exercised with bodily Illness; but still supported under it. And some-times enabled to rejoice in it. To see that 'tis best and can acquiesce in the Will of God. But alass! My remaining corruptions make me repine against God at times—I find a Law in my Members warring against the Law of my mind and bringing me into Captivity to the Law of Sin and Death!

O Lord Jesus! Thou are the captain of my salvation, Undertake for me [and] bring my will into subjection to thy most Blessed Will. I desire to be saved from the Power of Sin as well as from the Guilt of it. Lord! Compleat the work of salvation which I hope is begun in me and carry it on to Perfection!

DECEMBER 31, 1744
Monday

This Day we kept as a Family Fast; but how dead and stupid was I. When confessing Sin, how little was I humbled? While praying for Pardon, how faint and Languid where my desires after it? When asking for the spirit of God to enlighten and sanctifye Us, how little did I see my need of Him? While reciting the afflictions of the Year past, how unhumbled was I? When calling to remembrance the mercies of It, how unthankfull was I for them? When My Duty was pointed out to me, how unconcerned was I whether ever I practiced it? In fine, this whole day was spent in a formal manner by me.

JANUARY 25, 1745
Friday

I hope I can say that Yesterday was a blessed day to me; in the Forenoon I felt a relish for the truths of God which I heard Dr Sewall preach.[31] But the afternoon was a time to be peculiarly remembred by me. Bless the Lord, O my soul, for the manifestation of his Love which he vouchsafed me then. Mr Whitefield preached from 1 Thess. 1:4. I hope the blessed Spirit witnessed with mine that I was elected of God [and] *called* and so might know that I was *Elected* of God. I was fill'd with humble thankfullness and Joy in God [and] was astonished at his Condescending Love to me, the least, the most unworthy of Adams race. I was then from *Gratitude* resolved that I would do my utmost in the strength of Christ to live up to my Holy Calling, to give up My self intirely to him, [and to] obey his Dying Precent [Precedent?] by comming up to his Table. O Lord! Suffer me not to fall from these resolutions.

Eve
While my Father was reading his text this *Eve*, Isa. 57:15, I beheld something of the *greatness* of the high and lofty one that inhabiteth Eternity, whose name is *holy* and who dwells in the high and holy place. His Greatness [and] His Holiness shone forth in these Words with a peculiar Glory. I was amazed that he shou'd take notice of such Worms of the dust as we are. And especially that he shou'd condescend to *Dwell* with them, Wonderfull Grace indeed![32] May I allways live in the realizing sence of it!

JANUARY 29, 1745
Tuesday

Mr W[hitefiel]d preach'd from Matt. 18:3, and I hope the Blessed Spirit wittnessed with my spirit that I was Converted and become a little child; and "O, that I was more humble, more meek, and lowly was the Desire of my soul!" What a sweet peace have I felt this A.M. Surely their is a sweet peace in believing! Blessed be my dear Saviour. I hope I know what it is by Experience! I long to have every one Acquainted with Christ. I want all to experience the power of Godliness. I want all to know the Love of Christ which passeth knowledge.[33] O Lord, do thou say Amen and it shall be so! Thou are able to create them all anew in thy self. O, do it I beseech thee, My Lord, and My God! I know not how to leave pleading with God 'till he rains down righteousness on his backsliding people.[34] But this is my Comfort: that I have a tender hearted, mercifull, and prevalent intercessor at Gods right hand. And therefore I leave it with him.

MARCH 17, 1745
Sunday

How different am I now from what I was a few weeks agoe? Then I cou'd delight in God, but now I have no veiw of his amiableness. Then my Meditation was chiefly on heavenly Things, now on Earthly—Then I had some recrross [recourse] to God in prayer, But now I am at a distance from him, Quite formal and lifeless!

> "Why is my heart so far from Thee,
> "My God, my chief delight?
> "Why are my Thoughts no more by Day,
> "With thee no more by night?
> "Why shou'd my foolish passions rove?
> "Where can such sweetness be?
> "As I have tasted in thy Love,
> "As I have found in thee?"
>
> Watts[35]

I desire to lay the blame on My self and Justifye God in all his dealings with me. He is Unchangable, but I have Sinned against his Love. O, that he wou'd humble me and bring me to lay at his foot, and accept of him as my Sanctifier, as well as Comforter. Amen.

From hence My Journal is contain'd in other Papers untill January 1, 1756, when I began at the other End of this Book.[36]

Memorandum
[Undated]

In summer 1755 at the sacrament solemnity, was sung part of Rev. [. . .] upon which I had such ravishing views of the Glory which will redound to Christ from the salvation of his People and such raised veiws of the Preciousness of *that Blood* which cou'd avail to Wash such a Multitude of horrid Filthy sinners and make 'em white that I desire if ever a sermon be made on my death, It may be from those Most Lovely Words Rev. 7:14 "*These are they* which (came out of great tribulation and) *have washed their robes* and made them White in the *Blood of the Lamb*." Surely as 'tis added, this must be the cause why they are admitted to all the Glories following in the 15, 16, 17 ver[ses]: 'Tis not the *Merit* of *their* greatest sufferings, nor of *their* Best Services that procures them, But the *Blood of the Lamb!* To *that* I flee, on that alone I depend for cleansing, pardon, acceptance, and all My salvation, and to that will I for ever ascribe the Whole. Amen.

JANUARY 1, 1756
Thursday

I desire to give My self to the Lord in a perpetual Covenant—I trust I have done it this Morning—I long to Live to God entirely and do more for him than Ever, more for Others than Ever. I long to have all my time and tallents Us'd in his Service!

Eve
Had a quiet, resigned temper of mind this day and desire to wait on God for all Salvation, temporal and spiritual. Reciev'd a remarkable Answer of Prayer. Felt some Gratitude.

JANUARY 3, 1756
Saturday Eve

I can't but hope God has begun a work of Grace in my heart, but I want more of his Image. I long to get near to him and have close Communion with him—I want to cleave to him and abide in him.

JANUARY 4, 1756
Sunday

I trust I had some delight in the day and Ordinances—and some outgoings of heart after God—and felt Longing desires to serve him—and essay'd to renew my Covenant with him at his Table and in Private—But O, how faint, how sluggish, how cold are my affections; I loath My self! Lord enliven, quicken, pardon, and sanctify me for the dear Sons Sake. Amen.

JANUARY 10, 1756
Saturday

I have such a fountain of sin still in me—My heart is so vain, worldly, and sensual as makes me fear I am not a Real christian—I am in perplexity about My state. I trust it is my hearty desire that God wou'd search me and try me and not let me retain one Idol but seperate me from all sin and make me to relinquish every thing for him—Lord, give me thy self, and I will be Content tho' I am stript of all Other things.

Eve
Spent a Considerable part of this day in Prayer, Reading, and Examination in Order to solemn Covenanting with God which I longed to do with all my heart—I read over one form and another, which in former Seasons I thought I closed deliberately and heartily with, and I cou'd rejoice in the Thought of being Bound to the Lord in indissoluble ties—But I was afraid I was not intirely sincere—I fear'd a decietfull heart and lest there was some reserve hidden from me but known to God—I therefore Earnestly and frequently Cried to him to make me sincere; and if I was Unwilling to be for him intirely, I intreated him to Make me Willing—I felt my spiritual impotency and that I cou'd not Open my heart to him—But I earnestly beg'd him to Open My Soul and enter in and Reign in me and destroy all my Lusts and make me holy—I Laboured to yeild My self and all My Enjoyments and Prospects and Concerns to his absolute dispose; and so far as I know my heart (but I dare not trust it 'tis so decietfull), I desired to relinquish all sin and all Creatures and be and do and Suffer any thing to have him for my Portion—I dare not say I am sure I surrendred My self to him; but I tried to do it and so far as I know my heart, I assented to

31

that in Mrs Rowes Devout Exercises and made it my own Deed Entitled "a surender of the Soul to God" No. 31. Page 126.[37] I laboured to sacrifice my most desireable comforts and Prospects to God and to have My Will brought to nothing [so] that the Lords Alone may be Exalted—O, my God, make me Thine—Make me like thee, Be Mine, and I have Enough!—This, This is all I crave, and I must Lay at thy Foot and Cry 'till I gain this Blessing of Blessings. Lord I must be thine, I cant be Easy with out Thee—I must, and by thy Grace assisting, I will follow hard after Thee!

JANUARY 11, 1756
Sunday

A.M.: Felt determined to press after God as a Portion. P.M.: Unwatchfull and Carnal but loath'd My self.

JANUARY 12, 1756
Monday

Have recievd Much Mercy in Outward Comforts these 12 days past; and when I was greatly press'd with Outward Trials Dec[ember] 31, I was brought to resign to God and Cast all on him and Leave all with him to dispose just as he saw meet—Now I find he did not reject my poor Cries nor turn a deaf Ear to My Groans—I have reaped so largely in answer to Prayer As Astonishes me! I felt some Gratitude leading me to Praise him from whom all bounties flow. Here I sit up a witness that 'Tis Good to trust God, Pray, and wait and quietly hope for all Needfull salvations, a Witness that God is good to the soul that seeks him. And that 'Tis good to record his Mercies!

FEBRUARY 21, 1756
Saturday

O, my Leaness, My sensuallity, and stupidity—I feel guilty and confounded at what a low, very low, rate do I live. Methinks I am less than the Least![38] Yea, I fear I grow less than I ever was in the christian Life!—I make no advance! O, to be brought near to God and made conformable to him—God has graciously show'd himself to me the week past, A *hearer of Prayer*. 'Tis a Loud call to Gratitude and Love and engagedness of heart in his Service. O, help me, Lord, to Live thy Praises and call on Thee as Long as I Live—He now allso gives me to wait on him for the Accomplishment of a Promise, which has occasioned Me Many uncommon Exercises (*as noted in a distinct diary*) and great perplexity for Many Months; and now he apears to give me a confirming time and to see that he is the Performer as well as giver of Promises.[39]

MAY 20, 1756
Friday

Was seiz'd with a violent Nervous Fever—At First did not aprehend Danger—Felt desirous that God might be glorified by this Illness—Was very Calm. I humbly hope the spirit of God witness'd with mine that I was a Child of his—And I felt a Rest on his imutable Covenant and Promises—Not one doubt, not one Fear, not one Care?—No desire to Live or die? Or, to know which was apointed, but I Left all with God—'till Sunday, *May 30*. Then I saw the Openings of Eternity—It was a solemn Thing to Enter into the presence of God, but still I hop'd in the Righteousness of the slain Lamb—I cou'd look back on solemn Covenant Dedications to God and on other Transactions with him with Abundant Comfort—And I was sure I chose to be his Living as well as Dying. My Reason was Clouded so that there seems to be an inconsistency in my Frames and Ideas—*From that Day* my Fever Abated and when I found God call'd me Back from the Gates of Death, O, how did my very heart pant to Glorify him! How did I long to dissolve with Thankfulness, how Glorious did his truths, his Ways, a Life of Strict Piety, and close walking with him apear. How amicable his Sabbaths, his Ordinances, [and] his People apear. I never felt a greater Union with and Love to his children who Ever bore his Image; of all Parties and thro' the whole World, I lov'd. How did I long for the increase of his dear Kingdom; it apear'd more desirable than any thing else, yea, to be my chief joy.

JULY 18, 1756
Sunday

What, O my soul, are thy desires—and What thy fix'd choice? To be resolved only as to these Queries is a Matter of Moment—Canst thou say I desire Christ and his Grace—[that] I desire the subduction of my Lusts—[that I desire] Conformity to Gods Holy Law—[that I desire] Victory over the World to Live to God; [that I desire to] Obey and Glorify him [and that] I desire Nearness to and Communion with him and that these are the chief, the strong, the prevalent desires of my Soul?

Ponder well the Answer—And see if this is the Case?—And why thou desirest these—To these things help me, O my God, sincerely to reply!—So far as my heart is known to me, I feel Unsatisfied and uneasy with out these Upper sparing Mercies; and I hope I am pursuing after them from Year to Year and Month to Month and Week to Week—I see a transcendent Beauty in them—This makes me desire 'em. See all other things are vain in their duration and empty in their Nature—This makes me desire them—I feel such an Inward emptiness in my self that with out them I can't be happy. This makes me desire them—Was there no future state, I think I wou'd desire these things here as the only Good that cou'd satisfye me.

As to my choice, the objects presenting are as set in contrast

God the glorious One	Creatures
Holiness	Sin
Grace	The power of lust in me and gratification of 'em
Comunion with God and the Influences of his Spirit	Sensual enjoyments, Worldly Comforts, Riches, Honours pleasures—to the full
The Light of his Countenance and tokens of his Love	Flatteries and smiles and favours of All Men
Wittness of his Spirit	Worldly fame—Reputation Character, etc.
The Cross of Christ, self denial, Reproach of Men. Contempt and Scorn and Ill-Usage, Affliction, sickness, Sorrow, poverty, etc.—with a Good Conscience, the favour of God and comforts of Religion.	Prosperity, Self-gratification, Health, Outward Peace—Plenty—A full Table—fine aparell—Delicacies and Grandures of Life With a heart void of true Grace.

Again, Pause, Consider Well, and then answer, Which is thy free, full, deliberate, serious choice? So far as I know my heart I have made choice of God for My Portion—His Grace for my Riches—His holy Religion for my happiness—Have renounced Sin—The World and My Carnal Self have seen Such an Infinite Amiableness in the One Object and such an emptiness and deformity in the other as to make me prise and choose the One, hate and renounce the Other—(O! that I may not deceive my self in this) and I humbly trust all this has been wrought in me by the Working of Allmighty Power and Grace!—One thing I know—That once 'twas other wise—Was a stranger to all the Lovliness of this Grand object. But I cant deny this; I have been always a stranger, for I do know I have seen such a Beauty in it as has made all created Beauty, the World, and all in it Vanish into Shades of *God; the Infinite God* has apeared to be *the all in all*—Time's, Sweet times have been when I wou'd have despised the offer of Worlds for my portion and Why this? Because I panted for God, I choose him for my portion and was resolved I wou'd take up with nothing short of him— The World has offered its charms. Satan and my Lusts have enticed me to accept—But with a superior Ardor I have rejected. The past two months— Yea, this very day wittnesses for me that I reject, with pleasure reject, all the offer of Worldly riches and pleasures—[. . .] tho' my carnal heart sides—Tho' these are considerable inducements to [. . .]—I will not— Least God, my Glorious Maker and Redeemer, be dishonored and because I fear 'twill draw me from him—With all my heart I desire to renew my choice this day and take the Blessed God, the Father, Son, and Spirit for my Portion—His Laws for my Rules, his Religion for my happiness, his Glory for the End to which I aim and desire his spirit to dwell in [and] Rule and Guide and Sanctifye me, his People for my People—To accept of his Son as my Compleat saviour, renouncing my own righteousness. Take up his Cross and through a hard[40] path of steady obediance and Patient suffering follow My Blessed head and Great Exemplar, 'till sin be done quite away on me and perfect Holiness take place for ever!

Eve
A Glorious Day of the Son of Man has this been to me? The Prayers, Sermon, Sacrament, [and] season, all Mounts (as it were) of Transfiguration under the Sermon in which a Glorious Christ was displayed in his Personal and Mediational Excellencies—His Communicative fullness, his indearing Offices—He apeared to me Infinitely Precious, all together

Lovely. He drew me and I willingly ran after him—I trust I had the seal-ing and Wittnessing of his Spirit—At one time, as the Minister was say-ing that the Unbelievers Language was "We will not have this Man to reign over Us," My very heart cried I choose and will have This God Man to reign absolutely, supreamly, and Eternally over me.

At the Lords Table I was brought into the banqueting house, and Christ's banner was Redeeming Love—With great delight I sat Under his Shadow, and most sweet was the fruits of his Purchase—He offered himself and his Grace to me—He Opened My heart to accept the offer, and he helped me to give My heart and My all to him—O, happy, happy Exchange. Language can't describe my then veiws or what I thought of his Amazing Love and Grace to me—This one thing I will add, that I then thought I wou'd not relinquish the blessed Bargain for ten thousand Worlds!—Notwithstanding all this, I saw eno' to humble me to the dust, for I saw I had yet a Body of Sin in me—A heart prone to go astray from God—Wandring and vain and unwary, I groned for deliverance from Sin and for Compleat Sanctification—I saw I shou'd never be perfectly holy here, and this made me rejoice in the hope of dying—I solaced my self with the Prospect of that perfection taking place in that Holy, happy State and then with believing desires and full Expectation waited for and hastned to—I rejoiced in that God wou'd be then Glorified by me—O, how amicable were the day the house and all the Ordinances of my God!—Surely this was a Halcyon day! Allmost a Pencil![41] Praise the Lord—O, for a Circumspect Walk—May I keep my heart—Watch and Pray allways, Live near to and on Christ, my Glorious Head, and in his Strength Mortifye Lusts, Live [. . .] above the World, and go on my Way rejoicing! *At Noon* a precious season!

P.M. Unwatchfull!—O, what am I! After such enjoyments to wax cold is the most Base Ingratitude. O God, My God, Sanctifye me wholly in spirit, Soul, and Body; I beseech Thee for Jesus, my blessed Saviour and Interces-sors Sake. Amen.

JULY 29, 1756
Thursday

Under the Preaching of the Word, I humbly hope I had the sensible pres-ence of My Blessed Redeemer and the Wittness of his Spirit to my adop-tion, that I had such a Glimpse of his Glory as made all other things van-ish into shades—Christ and his Religion apeared to be all in all, worthy my attention, choice, and pursuit—I felt satisfied with my Portion and rejoiced in it more than in all Riches—Great have been my trials for 10 days past, but (wondrous Grace!) I am help'd to acquiesce. Yea, I feel well pleased with them because a Wise, a Holy, a Gracious Covenant God Orders them and adjusts their Manner, time, and Circumstances. I leave my all with him and I feel happy!

AUGUST 12, 1756
Thursday

Have Seen and Experienced much of the Kind Care of God in carrying me thro' and Extricating me from great trials and perplexity—To him be Glory—He has guided and delivered in all and let this encourage thee, O my soul, allways to Confide in him in all Cases.

> When troubles rise and storms apear
> To him I'll safely hide.
> God has a strong pavillion where
> He Makes my soul abide![42]

AUGUST 15, 1756
Sunday

Had some desires after the presence of Christ—Cou'd not feel Easy with out—Was Stupid and lifeless in the duties of Religion—But this was my Burden.

I cannot live Contented here with out some Glimpses of his Face. I hope I had some Grace in Exercises, tho' alass how Little! Lord, pardon and sanctifye me thro' the Blood of Atonement.

SEPTEMBER 12, 1756
Sunday

I see my bent to vanity. I feel a reluctance to Holiness. My heart is often rising up in secret disatisfaction with the Providence of God—O, My heart is hard—My will is stubborn. Yea, 'tis Obstinately stubborn—My affections are sensual, cleaving to Earth. I feel Guilty, and Yet I have not a penitent heart, a heart to mourn for this—I feel shut up. Can't pray with any Life—O, Miserable one that I am—Gloominess and Malloncholly have lately been Predominant. The Aspect of Providence both on Public, Private, and Personal Concerns apear dark indeed—But I fear the true spring of my dejection is an Undue Love to things below—The World, Friends, Comforts and pleasures of life, etc. So when it looks as tho' I should be deprived of them, My heart sinks—Wretched case—Lord, pity! And save me from my sinfull Self [and] My inbred Corruption! Pardon, purifye, and sanctifye for thy sons sake! And give me a transforming Glimpse of thy Glory this day, and that will deaden me to all things Else—Let me see the King in his Beauty, and that will Captivate my whole soul and do more towards sublimating My affections in one Moment than the most rational arguments and persuasive reasonings, the pomp of Rhetoric, and flow of Eloquence cou'd do in a thousand Years. O, Divine spirit! Thou Grand illuminator, Come and take of the things of Christ and show them to a poor Worm.

SEPTEMBER 19, 1756
Sunday

I have for some time been in great Perplexity with respect to a very interesting Affair.[43] The path of Duty is not plain, and I am in much concern—I have been deliberating seriously and solemnly—Have been consulting with Friends, but no help—I desire to be very thankfull for the following things: That God enables me to Consult Duty more than Inclination; That he helps me to Make his Glory My Governing Aim; That he helps me to resign to his Will and chuse to be ruled by it; That he takes off my dependance from My own Judgement and the Judgement of others, not leaning to my own Understanding but helps me to trust on him and constantly to comit my Ways to him; That he helps me to wait at his Foot for direction in his own time and way and makes me willing to follow just where he leads—I feel willing to have it ordered one way or the other just as it pleases him and resigning My self to him to dispose of absolutly, I now wait for the discovery of his Will [and] dare not decide for my self and dread nothing more than to be left to the Bent of my own heart.

Eve
I solemnly resigned my Case into the hands of Jesus, my Blessed Advocate with the Father.

OCTOBER 13, 1756
Wednesday

After Serious Deliberation, proper Consultation, and Solemn Prayer, I determined the affair and threw My self into the Arms of Mercy upon

which all My Anxiety Ceased; and to this Day, *vis* November 6, I feel perfectly well pleased that I did make that Determination.[44]

November 6, 1756
Saturday Eve

I feel very Stupid and Earthly, yet I can't say but I loath it and long for
Quickening Grace!

December 21, 1756
Tuesday

Altho' I am a poor, fruitless, barren, cold, sluggish Soul—Unstable as
Water, prone to go astray from God and have been very negligent of
Religion for some time past; Yet Amidst these decay[s] I have not been
with out some reviving [and] some pantings after God—Some access to
him through Christ and this day in particular I have found more true
pleasure in secret intercourse with Him and admiring views of him than
Ever I found in the World and all its Charms! Be thankfull, O my Soul, and
continue thy pursuits after Him, whose favour in Life, and whose loving
kindness thou knowest to be better than Life.

January 19, 1757
Wednesday 1 P.M.

Adored be the riches of free Grace. God has taken me near to him the
past Month—Given me some glimpses of his glory [and] some tastes of
his Love!

 I have been allowed sweet access to his Throne—I trust I have been
panting after him. As the hunted hart after the Water brooks, so have I
thirsted for God, Ever the Living God—I trust he has been with me in
secret, social, and Public Ordinances—Has drawn me and I have gladly
run after him. Yea, I have found his Gracious presence with me in the
Common Actions of Life—I trust he is earning on his Work in this heart
and as he gives me to wrestle with him for sanctification, so I can't but
hope he will fullfill those desires which he himself has created in me. Yea,
I believe he will, for Faithfull is he that hath Promised—He helps me to
follow on and know more of him—to a fixed determined Choice of
him as my *Portion*—to a frequent surrender of my All to him—to Ardent
breathings after Communion with him and Conformity to his *Nature* in

Habitual Holiness and Will in an active, Uniform, steady Obedience—
Nothing do I long for so much as to be all for God, to have my Soul
brought near to him, and to lay in a holy subjection to him, and to Live
and act entirely for him.

I rejoice that I was made for his Glory; I see it to be an End Worthy of
God—I see it to be the Felicity of my Nature that he made me capable of
being like him and bringing Glory to him, and I do delight In him with a
superlative Affection—I never felt that intense desire after Creatures which
I feel to the Blessed God—My soul thirsteth for him; it goes out in breathings after him—The dearest of creatures are nothing to me to what he is—
The best of Earthly society is empty to me [compared] to what secret
convene with my God [is]—And often has the Company of my dearest
Friends been burdensome because I have long'd to be alone to think more
intensely of him, to go more fully to his throne of Grace, and there
Converse more freely with him; and if I am not most awfully mistaken, I
wou'd not exchange one hour of Access to him in this little chamber for
Thrones of State—And as the Obstinacy of my Will has been one of the chief
Plagues I have groned Under for Many Months, so of late he has helped to
go to him to Cure it—He has given me to bewail it and to cry Abba Father,
All things are possible with thee.[45] Thou canst destroy this rooted Principle
of stubborness, and thy son has purchased this redemption for me, and
thou hast promised that Sin shall not have domminion over me—I depend
on thy Word, and I will not let thee go 'till thou bless me—'till thou
changest my heart so that all its breathings, all its desires, [and] all its
Prayers shall be comprized in this. Father, thy Will be done.

I can't rest 'till this is wrought, 'till my Will be broken, and God
alone be Exalted in me—I delight in the thought of sacraficing my All to
him and to have him Possess and rule me entirely; and I can't be Easy to
be only so now and then, but I want to be so continually—I long to be
allways swallowed up in him!—And to have a sincere respect to all his
Commandments—Not to regard one or many but all—I long to Love
him with all my heart and soul and to love my Neibour as My self[46]—
I see an amiableness in this his Law, and I long to be molded into the
image of it.

I want to do every common action after a Godly sort—to have a
supream aim at the glory of God in all I do, and therefore I desire to take
his Word for my rule as well as his Glory for my End. O my dear Redeemer,
Let me be Thine, and be thou mine; and rule and possess and fill me, and
I have all I Want. I am contented, Yea, more than contented. I am fully sat-

isfied and Well Pleased with My Portion. O [. . .] Free Grace! This shall be my song and this my Triumph to Eternity!

JANUARY 21 AND 22, 1757
Friday and Saturday 2 P.M.

Was brought into My self to see and feel my inbred Corruptions, and O, how amazing was the sight—With Job I felt that I am Vile, and I cou'd not express how Vile. Scarce was I ever so Burdened with the sence of Indwelling sin. My heart felt resigned to die within me, and I could do nothing but lay and grone out My burden, more by inexpressible thoughts than audible Ventings. Spent the day chiefly in secret prayer [and] cries for sanctification. I felt allmost distracted (Not from terrible Apprehensions of *Wrath* but) from *a conviction of my Extreem Contrariety to the Blessed God.* This so engaged and overwhelmed me that I cou'd not attend to any business conversation, etc. O, methinks I am the Vilest [and] stubbornest of all Flesh. Never did any make so little progress in Sanctification as I. I loath and abhor My self and desire to be broken to pieces and lay low at the Foot of Christ, all my life beging for Holiness.

JANUARY 23, 1757
Sunday

O, the Wonders of the Religion of Christ! His Ways are all Wonderfull to me—Yesterday and this day my heart thirsted, [and] my Flesh cried out for the Living God. Ever to see his Glory and feel his Power as I have seen him in his Sanctuary. I trust he was graciously near me in secret and Private Duties and led me to wrestle and take no denial for a Blessing on his Ordinances, and now this Evening *I wittness for him* that he is near to the soul who seeks him and never fails those who humbly trust in and choose him. *This one day* in his house has been better than a Thousand Else where. For tho' I never saw my own *emptiness* and *Vileness* more clearly, yet I felt inexpressible delight. For O! I saw something of the Infinite Amiableness of the Divine Redeemer, in his Personal Glory and Lovelyness of his mediational character! I saw him Worthy to be Loved and served, and I rejoiced that he is *God over all,* blessed for ever. The Nature of Gracious Subjection to him was opened, and my heart Echoed to every Word—I can't but hope the blessed spirit witness'd with mine that I did thus kiss the son, and all my grief was that [I] was not Entirely subject to him. Thus God dealt with

41

a vile, sinfull worm! O, I want to Lay allways at his Foot mourning my unlikeness to him and beging for his Image to be instampt on my whole Frame!—This body of sin is my burden—To think that I shall sin against this Glorious One again [and] to think that my wretched heart will run away from him again; This depresses me. O, for holiness [and] heart Purity—O, for a New bent. O, to be entirely subject to God. Dear redeemer, I thirst for this. O my King, thou art my Lord! Where is any other that can save me from this Worst of Evils, sin? I flee to thee to subdue me.

"Great God create my soul anew"
"Conform my heart to thine"
"Melt down my Will and let it flow"
"And take the mold divine"
"Siese my whole frame into thine hands"
"There all my Powers I bring"
"Manage the Wheels by thy Command"
"And govern ev'ry Spring"
"Then shall my Feet no more depart"
"Nor wandring senses rove"
"Devotion shall be all my heart"
"And all my Passions Love"[47]

O, to be fix'd fast to Thee. Such a confinement wou'd be Liberty itself.

JANUARY 24, 1757
Monday

I hope [I] had the Presence of Christ in secret duties and was help'd in some degree to keep watch over my heart thro' the day—Felt a distrust of my self and that kept me more dependant on him.

JANUARY 25, 1757
Tuesday

A.M.: Found my Predominent stirring and in order to get it more subdued, I purpose by divine help to set apart this afternoon for solemn, secret prayer for Victory over that and all sin and for Grace to help in all times of need—And as I find Much Stubborness of Will, much Sensuallity of Affections, Love to self, the World and Vain thoughts. Much Pride and very little spirituallity and that I need Much Purification, Light, and Grace and need constant Supplies from the fullness that is in Christ. I purpose (in his Fear and Looking to him for assistance and acceptance) to set apart two afternoons in a Week for the Exercises of *Secret Prayer* for all kinds of sanctification both in heart and Life—Self Examination and Meditation—Not to omit other common stated times but to take these from the World and Worldly business—And to keep to it for two Months from this day—And then as I shall see it duty to keep on or not—And to make the Interest of Christs kingdom a part of my Errand—I also purpose to read over with Prayer Christs sermon on the Mount Every Monday Morning and beg that the spirit of it may be wrought into the texture of my heart that so my Life may be squared by it[48]—And all these I propose to the end that I may live nearer to God this Year, Grow more in a Conformity to *him who is my Vital head* in all things, and so Live to the Praise of the Glory of his Grace, and be ripened for a state of Perfect Holiness and Compleat Happiness in his Presence, Who is the all in all to his own People and whom I choose for my God and My all—O, Lord, I depend on thee for Grace so to wrastle as to obtain the Blessing—I also look to thee so to order things as I may have time and Liberty and a heart to Practice these resolves—The Preparation of the heart in Man and the Answer of the Tongue are Both from the Lord, and he never said seek my Face in Vain—This is my Warrant: Heb. 4:16, Eph. 6:10, [and] Luke 11:9–14; and this my Encouragement: John 16:23 [and] 1 John 8:14.[49]

Eve

I set to my seal that God never calls to duty but he affords strength to perform—The beginning of the P.M. I feared my unresolved heart wou'd weary, but I found Christ graciously to assist me and so to keep my heart fix'd as that it was a Lovely season and I tho't the time short—I do hope God help'd me to seek him sincerely—I had freedom to pour out my secrets to him and got leave to plead for my self, My Parents, the Family, My own Dear Ministers, the dear church I belong to, My Particular Friends—All in Affliction [and] Temptation, [also] The Town—Its churches—Its Ministers, The Land, its Ministers, churches, Magistrates, Lord Loudon—The Nation, The King—all his Ministers of state, Parliament, Officers, all his subjects, the church, Mr Whitefield, the Protestant Nations—Poor Protestants in France and Else-where—The whole church Militant—Yea, all the World and for the reign of Christ on Earth—Happy, happy Priviledge and now I will wait for thy Salvation, O God.[50]

JANUARY 29, 1757
Saturday 4 P.M.

Was help'd to spend the afternoon agreeable to the above Purposes—And tho' I was Cold and Dull In desire and Prayer, Yet I trust it was not a vain thing that I spent it thus—Was enabled to plead for the special Presence of Christ tomorrow—In his house and at his Table that there he will come as a *Conqueror* to destroy sin in me and even that he wou'd slay my *Predominant*. I beg'd that I might feel his mighty Power in bearing down my Lusts—Subduing my Enmity to his Laws—And disafection to his Providence and Will and that my whole soul might experience the purifying Efficacy of his Blood—Was also help'd to plead for others as in the foregoing Page—I can't but hope the spirit of God graciously assisted a Nothing Worm! O, I find 'tis a Pleasant Way of spending time!—I love it!

JANUARY 30, 1757
Sunday

I hope I had the presence of Christ with me. At the Lords Table I Laboured to bring forth My Darling Sin to be slain—and Essayed to renew Covenant Engagements to be the Lords wholly—To Love, Obey, and Please him and to Warr against Sin, all Sin, and the sin that most cleaves to me—I hope I cou'd hate and abhor my self and tho't I long'd for the Crucifixion of my Lusts.[51] But O, what stupidity, what insensibillity reign'd in me. O, 'tis astonishing!

Eve
Felt my Predominant stirring and gaining ground but presently was fill'd with shame and lay and groned out my burden before the Lord—I can't describe how I was oppress'd—But I went to my Blessed Advocate and got Liberty to vent my grones into his gracious Ear, and He was graciously pleased to *Lighten my heart by Faith* [and] *acted on his Intercession* for me, and a happy serenity ensued.

JANUARY 31, 1757
Monday A.M.

Found my heart vain and carnal and unwatchfull and had a strong conflict with sin—I felt so oppressed that I cou'd not make Language of my case but was help'd to try to Look to Jesus to make me Pure, meek, Lowly, [and] Mercifull. I feel a dreadfull Load on my Mind, no Faith, Love, [or] Humillity—I feel awful stubborness of Will and Carnality of affections, and it seems to me I get little or no victory over sin. Satan and my heart tempt me to desist trying and praying for Amendment, for that 'tis in hipocrisy and does no good—But I desire to hold on using *all means*, tho' *depending* on *none*; but all my hopes are founded on the Merits of Christ as the purchase and the Workings of his Spirit as the grand Efficient of my Whole Salvation from the power of Sin.

FEBRUARY 2, 1757
Wednesday 5 P.M.

Found a great backwardness and when I began, much straitness—But soon got some Freedom at the throne of Grace [and] was burdened with indwelling sin—O, this Body of sin! It more and more opresses me. I had near the close of the P.M. some sweet views of the Perfection of Holiness in the other World, and my soul Long'd for a deliverance from this Body. And with sweet delight I thought of Death or what wou'd bring about this. And Even Judgement Look'd desirable, for I had charming Views by Faith of the saints [and] their shining in the Beauties of Holiness and Christ as their admired head presenting the Whole Body, a Glorious church unto himself with out spot or Blemish, and all their Holiness, all their Felicity, as the Purchase of his own Blood. And O! if I may be one, tho' the smallest member, of that Body, 'tis my whole desire—These views comforted me to think a time wou'd come when the redeemed of the Lord will part with sin forever. O my Blessed Jesus, To thee my soul ascends in Earnest desires.

> Be thou my Pattern; make me bear
> More of thy gracious Image here;
> Then God, the Judge, shall own my Name
> Amongst the Followers of the Lamb[52]

FEBRUARY 5, 1757
Saturday

Prevented by Illness.

FEBRUARY 8, 1757
Tuesday 6 P.M.

Found great deadness, and as Pharoahs chariots went about the duty heavily, yet thro' grace pass'd thro' my backwardness and hope I had some sincerity.[53] Lord, Pardon thro' the Blood of atonement the sins of holy Duties and for thy own Name sake, hear my poor requests for Resignation and conformity to thee!

FEBRUARY 9, 1757
Wednesday

Had more sensible Access to the throne of Grace than yesterday[54]—and I trust somewhat of a child like temper and cou'd ask with Earnestness, humillity, and resignation. Wait and Look for an Answer of this P.M. Petitions—Nothing is too hard for the Lord—He saies and it is done; he commands and it stands fast, and none can possibly resist his Will—Remember 'Tis a God thou prayed to, an Unchangeable God.

FEBRUARY 12, 1757
Wednesday 7 P.M.

Found some delight in the exercises of Devotion—Tho' I felt great obstinacy of will, I felt as a stone—Hard as adamant and sometimes was on the point of giving over prayer, for corruption[s] seem to retain their Vigor; but then the Words of Christ encouraged me (Luke 18:1, 7, 8) to hold on—And I was enabled to plead for the destruction of sin in me and for Universal Holiness in habit and exercise. I felt greatly oppress'd with sin in my heart [and] for particularly want of Resignation to God's Will in all things—I long'd to make a free, full, Absolute surrender of every thing (Especially those things that my heart are most glewed to) to God so as never more to desire any thing but what he wou'd have me desire, nor chuse, nor Esteem, nor love but what he wou'd have me, and just as and just so much as he wou'd have me—And in all things to be subject to him. I long'd to sacrafice my dearest delights, hopes, and Prospects to him—and to be swallowed up in his Will to rejoice cheifly in his Glory that he is God. Blessed forever to rejoice that he does what he pleases with all his Creatures and with me in particular—That nothing can resist his Will, thwart his design, frustrate his councels—O, I long'd to have no Will of my own but to have his Will my settled choice and from thence to have it the genuine

46

Language of my heart. *Father, not* as I will but as thou Will't! For these things I continued pleading the bigger part of the afternoon and then spread the case of the Family, Church, Town, Land, Nation, and Protestant Interest, King, Nobles, Naval, Military and Civil rulers—King of Prussia—Persecuted Protestants, Friends, [and] Ministers of Christ Every where before God and got freedom to pray for 'em; and here I was eas'd of that Load.[55] I 'till then felt—For tho' I am ever so distress'd for my self, yet I find Ease and pleasure in Intercession for the Zion of God—O! I depend on the Intercession of Christ; not on my own, for my best duty is specious Sin!

Eve

Got much refreshment in reading Mr Brainerds Diary, For I can't but say My Fears, My Sorrows, My hopes, my Joys, my happiness, my desires, [and] my conflicts are described in what he felt from time to time; and when I find others who were far better than I had the same Corruptions, Fears, and Deficiencies to grapple to with as I—it encourages me to hope that I also shall get the Victory thro' Jesus, their and my saviour.[56]

Once they were mourning here below and Wet their couch with tears.[57] They wrestle hard as I do now with sins and doubts and fears. I ask them whence their Victory came. They with united voice [and] Breath ascribe their conquest to the Lamb [and] Their Triumph to his Death! And thus thro' his Blood I hope to come off Conqueror, too.

FEBRUARY 13, 1757
Sunday

Confined by Illness but happily found that God confines not his special Presence to Public Ordinances—Found some engagedness of heart to holy Duties—Some clear sense of the Nature of real Mortification and heart holiness, and I trust was strengthened in my spiritual Warrfare and thro' Christ more steadily determined in the prosecution of my Great Work—Some Earnest longings after holiness and willing to take arduous pains to attain it and Yet never saw more clearly that I can do nothing, but since Christ has promised to work in me to Will and to do (and that of his meer Grace) I chuse to labor in his strength, to Work out my salvation with Fear, etc.—Had some nearness to God in secret Prayer and some spiritual Views of him as a holy, Gracious, Wise sovereign, True, Unchangeable Being—The day was too short for me—How delightfull is this holy day! 'Tis the best of all the Week—O my God, let every Sabbath be as this, a faint emblem of Heaven.

FEBRUARY 14, 1757
Monday

I see I must be more vigourous; I am ashamed of my slothfullness—O, to be fervent in spirit and Constant in Working. Much there is to do in this heart—Sin is never Idle in me, and shall Grace Lie dormant? O my soul, Watch and Pray allways!—Find my Account in reading Christs sermon on the Mount each Monday Morning 'tis an Excellent means.

FEBRUARY 17, 1757
Thursday Eve

Have gone thro' a distressing P.M. At first felt Exceeding Guilty and filthy before God and felt as a Beast for stupidity, Enmity, Carnality, etc. Was disordered in My Animal spirit and this with a distresing sense of sin and a Felt distance from God all meeting together wrought an inconceivable Confusion and anguish—At first I cou'd not continue but a few minutes at a time in prayer—But I felt so distracted I must leave off—Then came the tempter to persuade me to put it off 'till another time; but I feared if I did, Satan wou'd gain advantage, and so I resolved to try to press after God and crying to him for help—And I felt some help before I closed; I trust was enabled to pray with some sincerity for my own Conformity to God and for the Flourishing of Christs Kingdom on Earth—and that I laboured to make a sacrifice of all my Lusts to Christ and to make an offering of my Will, affections, and whole soul to him—And nothing do I so much desire as to have sin rooted out of me, and the Image of the Holy God implanted in me and to be intirely subject to the Whole Preceptive Will of God, and allso to resign to and acquiesce in all his disposing will concerning me—I want to Yeild entirely to his Government with out so much as one reservation, no, not of the dearest Enjoyment but Yeild all to him. 'Tis the Contrary to this that is all my Unhappiness—Was I entirely fix'd in my affections on God, every thing wou'd come right to me—For I should love [and] rejoice in all he does.

FEBRUARY 18, 1757
Friday

In the morning felt at a distance from God! I see I am carnal, and I long more for heart purity—[and] The Presence of Christ and to live devoted to the Blessed God and have my lusts mortifyed than I do to enjoy any

Creature Good! I feel I am Unable to govern my thoughts one Moment—
They will fly off from God—I feel wretched on this account, and I think
I can be willing to endure Conflicts, trials, and Temptations if I may but
be more purged from Sin and Weaned of the World and made more holy
and brought nearer to God by them—Otherwise those spiritual Conflicts
I frequently have are so unspeakably distressing that nature shrinks when
I think of enduring *one more*—I have undergone more spiritual distress the
Last two Years by far than in all my Life before—And many times to that
degree that I was allmost distracted and [my] nature [was] ready to
sink—And when I think how little I am made better by all, I feel discouraged and ready to Conclude that my soul is the stubbornest that ever was
and needs more and rougher means to break and humble and subdue it
than ever any did and feel afraid that I make no progress in holiness at
all—O, that I might have the presence of Christ this day and that he wou'd
come and subdue Lust and Conquer my Will and reign unrivall'd in my
whole soul—I can't bear to live at a distance from God—I can't be satisfied with out him—'Tis Impossible for the whole World to satisfy my
Longings—'Tis *divine* Presence and Grace I long for!

Thro' the day felt oppress'd with a Load of Indwelling sin and frequently was on my knees beging for holiness but was much straitned and
distress'd with my own sloth and want of Faith and Freedom—At Dusk I
again retired and vented my Grief in Prayer—I opened my heart to God
and panted for his Law to be written on my heart. Got some Access to him
and cou'd apeal to him "that I chose his Favour, his Image, a life of
Communion with and devotedness to him and was seriously willing rather
to part with all the World than be destitute of these Spiritual Blessings. That
I wou'd not be contented with out himself and had much rather live in a
Cave in the most desolate Willderness with his Presence than be Sovereign
Mistress of the Globe with out his Favour and deliverance from my
Lusts"—O, these Lusts. I think I cou'd freely die to get rid of 'em. I know
I hate 'em sincerely, and yet they still dwell and strive to reign in me; but
for victory over 'em, I will follow the throne of Grace Night and Day—and
that by the help of Christ, as long as I have a day to Live.

In the Eve the 4[th chapter] of sol song was sweet to me—I wondred
to hear Christ say to such a loathsome, vile, forlorn creature that sins every
moment and has a fountain of sin within me *"Behold thou art fair; there is no
spot in thee."*[58] Sure tho't I, it can't be to me, such a sinfull and sinning heart
as mine! But then I took it that where any soul is united to him, it is
cloathed with *his righteousness* and *that* he beholds with a peculiar pleasure;

that is the meaning of *Fair*—But then I was at a loss how he cou'd say *"there is no spot in thee"* since I am all impure within—But methought he call'd me to come with him from *Amana,* the top of Shenir Lebanon, Lyons dens, etc.[59] Come by Faith and take a view of the heaven I am now preparing for you; don't allways pore on the darkness of the present state, but solace yourself with glorious views of the aproaching state I design for You and will prepare you for; I have begun to purifye you in the work of renovation; then I implanted a vital Principle of Holiness in you and that is reaching after a perfection of Holiness agreable to its Nature; it will (under my care) thrive and grow and in one happy Moment (*vis* at Death) arive at perfection. I now behold you with tender pity, groaning under your Burden of sin. These groans are a part of my Work in delivering you. I see all your distress [and] all your secret struggles. I behold my Image in You with delight, and in due time I shall fully deliver you; the Work now wrought is a part of *that* which I will make *perfect*; and therefore tho' I am displeased with sin in you and hide my Face and chasten you, yet I behold no spot in you so as utterly to reject you. No, every spot shall be wiped away by the Virtue of my Precious Blood, and I will Blot out all Your sins, and then you shall be holy and happy in My service and Presence forever!—Thus refreshing was these thoughts to me, and O, I long for the hastning of that thrice blissfull Period.

"Earth vanishes with all the charm it has in store"
"Its snares and gay temptations are no more"[60]

Come, Lord Jesus, Amen!—I feel happier since these views; they've eased me! More than if I had heard I had [. . .]

February 19, 1757
Saturday

In the Morning felt some desires after God and holiness—Met with a tryal of some unkind and unchristian treatment from One who makes a high Profesion of Religion and is fair in professions of Love to my Face, but behind my back insinuates false things of me—At first this decietfull treatment roiled and grieved me, but soon I was to see 'twas to prove whether I was sincerely Willing to take up the Cross.[61] (the very Cross God orders for me [and] whether I wou'd stand to the Articles). Last Evening consented, too, to give up *all* for God, Friendship, Reputation, as to be willing to be despised, villified, slandered, and ill us'd—I was led to carry it to God and pray for Grace so to do, for Grace to shake hands with the World and embrace reproach and hard treatment from *any*, with a meek lamblike Christ-like Temper—I cou'd not rest 'till I cou'd heartily Forgive that Person and cry'd to God to Forgive her and to make her more holy and Christ-like—I saw much of the Wisdom of God in ordering this tryal this very day, and my soul bless'd him for it—This cup my heavenly Father gave me and he help'd me to drink it.

10 P.M.

Spent in Prayer—Had something of the presence of Christ thro' the whole [and] Freedom of access in prayer—Felt a tenderness of Spirit—Great Love to all this World—Love to Enemies and such as had most injured me and cou'd lay and plead for holiness for them—Long'd and panted and with a Child like reverence and Confidence of Faith cou'd continue to plead for Universal holiness for My self—Sin, secret sin, apeared odious, and my soul tenderly mourn'd that I had sin dwelling in me—I long'd and beg'd for Meekness and Love and Universal Forbearance and Charity—O Lord (I cry'd), let me be holy and live to thee and have thy presence, and I have all I want—Felt more dead to all creatures than for a long while and long'd to be wholly dead. I trust that it was a happy P.M. Felt earnest desires to depart and be with Christ that I might be *perfectly holy* and serve him constantly with out any Imperfection—Felt a temper to say with respect to the *Greatest tryal I ever met with*, "Father I choose that thy Will take place of mine"[62]— After I had done, felt afraid of a carnal heart and of being unwatchfull and saw the importance of keeping strict watch over my heart If I wou'd attain to any spirituality; and so I set about Meditation on the Example of Christ in Suffering and endeavoured to trace it thro' all steps from the Manger 'till he expired on the Cross—In this I was graciously assisted—As also in some meditation on the Wisdom of God in the Oeconomy of Providence and Grace. Here I was led into such views as made me willing God shou'd take his own way with me and lead me just where and into what difficulties he pleased. This I saw was the only road to my Eternal home—And I sweetly acquiesced in his Wise Guidance, and my soul rested in God. I put My self as clay into his hands to mold me into what shape he pleased so as I was but made Like him and fitted to Enjoy him in heaven by all.

FEBRUARY 20, 1757
Sunday

In the morning felt desires after the Presence of God and that I might keep the day [in] holy thought—Felt solemn and relish'd spiritual truths—Felt a greater spirit of Candor and gentleness toward Mankind than commonly I do—In the A.M. Public Prayer, was help'd to more engagedness of soul than I usualy do in public prayers—Long'd and felt greedy to catch and aply every spiritual truth—At Noon Felt afraid of loosing my solemnity and engagedness of soul, beg'd of God to help me to keep my heart, and was in some measure able to set watch on my Lips—Had christian and spiritual discourse with Friends and felt some earnest pantings for holiness. "O, to be holy, O! to be all devoted to God and to Live entirely to him!"—my soul cried to God. As a Friend in Prayer, gave thanks to God for Gifts and Graces he had conferred on me. I found my latent Pride and self confidence catch'd at it, and O, how awfull it seem'd—I felt afraid of indulging self and cried to God to humble me and keep me low at his Foot—I tho't to speak to Miss —— [to] never to do the likes again for my vile heart was a monste[r] of pride—But then I thought it was better to do it when we are alone, and this I did next day; to say so before Company might perhaps draw them to say more and so build up what can never be too low—Self.

FEBRUARY 21, 1757
Monday Morn

Again read my Weekly portion and I see (every time I read) farther of the Spirituallity, rectitude, Strictness, Extensiveness, and admirable Fittness of this Unchangeable rule of righteousness, and God enables me to accept of it for my rule; and I not only see 'tis right, but I hope I Love it because 'tis pure and reaches to the thoughts and intents, yea, to the most secret principles of the heart. Had some Enlargment, Engagedness, and solemn sense of God [and] of my own Inabillity to do any thing towards keeping this Law and was intense in supplicating him to write it on my soul—Was help'd to pray over what I had read and saw something of the Excellency of what I prayed for—After wards felt jealous of my heart least it turn off to Vanity—[.] S—— and C—— came in, C—— being going into the Country—We took leave, commending ourselves and each other in Praying together at which time I think my soul saw as clearly and penetrated as far into the Nature of Divine things—the Method of salvation [and] the nature and tendency of Grace in the soul and the worth and importance of it—as ever I did in my whole Life.[63] And my soul seem'd wholly to rely on God, and I felt I think more dead to every Creature, to self, and the World and to the dearest Friends I have than ever before. My

52

Happiness seem'd all to centre in God, [but if] my Will [is] to be swallowed up and lost in his, I cou'd not say. I had a choice for any thing in Life but left all with him—At the same time I saw my own Insufficiency to remain in his temper one Moment but *felt intirely dependant on Christ and rejoiced to feel so*—How sweetly solemn is an Awe of the Holy God—I was far from thinking [I] was mortified eno'; no, I long'd to be more mortified and to have no room in my heart but for God—Was my Bliss to serve him.

P.M.
Went abroad from a sense of Duty and to perform the Law of Christ in visiting one of his Sick Members but went with fear least my heart shou'd wander from God—Had some sweet tho'ts while abroad—But alass, I felt too too carnal [and] felt ashamed that I cou'd not live and act the Christian—Eve, came home that I might Labor to recall my heart and get near to God.

FEBRUARY 22, 1757
Tuesday

Had some serious sense of the Excellence of living to God—Felt uneasy that I did not live allways near to him—Got some engagedness of Soul in divine things in the Forenoon, but some sensual Objects were thrown necessarily in my way; and O, how empty did they seem, quite despicable— However, thro' Mercy my soul returned to its happiness—Felt jealous of my heart and was help'd frequently to retire for prayer, yet alass, I feel far from God!

Eve
Had some intenseness of Soul in Meditation on Gods Infinity, Eternity, *Unchangableness,* Wisdom, Holiness, Power, *justice, Goodness,* and Truth—Had some delightfull, new, and clear thoughts of his ever Unchangeable Blessedness [and] of his Justice and Goodness, and My soul delighted in him. In Evening Prayer felt ardent and increasing pantings after God and holiness and seem'd as if I cou'd not let him go 'till my Soul went and lodged its cause with Jesus and could leave it depending on his advocacy. After, felt Serene and Waiting for a gale from the Blessed Spirit—O, 'tis good to watch and pray allways!—Think I feel more weaned from Creatures than ever before and want nothing to make me happy but to have God all in all to me.

FEBRUARY 23, 1757
Wednesday

In the A.M. felt a small degree of spirituality—In the P.M. went into company and there I indulged My self in the most trifling Conversation—by which I greatly dishonoured God and his Religion which I have so openly professed and displeased the holy God who can't bear Evil [and] who perfectly hates Carnality!—O, how have I grieved his Spirit?—How grieved the dear redeemer? How set my self at a distance from God? And have provoked him to depart and he has departed from me; and I now feel a wretched stupidity and carelessness of Soul—I can justify God in leaving me. I see he is Perfectly just in punishing me—I can adore him for this very act of justice! But I can never feel happy while I am in this Carnal Temper—I know of no happiness but in being some (nay, engaged) in Love to the Blessed God or some resemblance of him—In being near to him and *walking with God humbly, Watchfully, Believingly*, [and] *holily* lies all the happiness I know of; and if I know nothing of these things in reality, then I have no happiness nor never had any. O, that My heart was properly affected with my Sin.

FEBRUARY 24, 1757
Thursday 11 P.M.

A.M. Was distressed with the Guilt of sin upon my conscience and Power of it on my heart, and God was offended! I felt I had provoked him to leave me, and I did and wou'd, yea, I lov'd to, ascribe righteousness to him. O, my Ingratitude [and] my baseness hung dismal before me, and I trust I felt sin the worst Evil—I tried one private and secret duty but cou'd get no access to God. Then I felt as a vile Beast before him—I went to his house to seek him, but I found him not; yet I was determined to seek him, sorrowing 'till I found him. O, how bitter is Sin, 'tis Gall and Wormwood![64] Yet I was astonished to find God Gracious notwithstanding all my sin, for the sermon was on Naamons Leprosy and Cure, and Spiritually applyed in the outward word to me.[65] Tho' I had not Faith to receive it, yet I saw God offered me Cleansing. I came home as one bowed down and wrote my heart in *Devout Misscellanies* and then spent the P.M. in Prayer, where I was help'd to a hearty Confession and I hope Genuine repentance and fresh flight to Jesus to his attonement, righteousness, Grace, Power, and Intercession. I got my load of Guilt laid over to him and then to a renewed hearty reliance on him, [then to] deep mourning that

54

I had dishonoured and *grieved him*, and then to clear perceptions of his Grace and salvation, and great Liberty to plead for cleansing and Sanctification and to continue to wrestle for my self, Family, Friends, My Ministers, Church, Town, Laws, Nation, Protestant Interest, whole Church Millitant, etc. 'till Dark; and I think if I ever discerned the Nature of Spiritual things, 'twas now. Felt more diffident of my own strength and Jealousy of my own heart and more engaged to Watch over my heart and tongue than Ever. O, I wou'd give a thousand Worlds never to sin more, in thought, in word, or in Deed.

FEBRUARY 25, 1757
Friday

In the morning felt desirous to be spiritually Minded—But ah! I foolishly went into vain conversation—And when I returned to duty, how full of vain tho'ts—I was Unhinged for everything, and Passion and Envy and pride and revenge worked. Remember this, O my Soul, and let it stand as a warning hence what thy carriage God['s] words ought to be in the Beginning of Every day!

This day had an onset from [. . .] the Bait [?] was a golden one—But with purpose of heart, I cleaved to the Lord as my Daily Portion.

FEBRUARY 26, 1757
Saturday

Much disordered in body attended with a Great depression of the Animal Spirits, but my Mind was clear and composed—Felt not that Fervor of affection in religious duties as I wanted to arive to because I wanted to be all ardor in Worshiping Him as he deserves to be served, with the height of pious affection—Felt a cleaving to him as my portion and a resignation to his will come sickness, come health, come Life, come Death. Every thing that God orders is Best for His Glory and for my best Interest—Felt desirous to be more weaned from Creatures and to know more of God and Love him more. Was deprived by a peculiar providence from being much in secret prayer, and O, how disagreable it seem'd only as God in his holy dispose permitted things to fall out. Thus I desired to resign it to him. I am amazed at my dullness in spiritual things! Lord, quicken me after thy word for thine own Name sake.

FEBRUARY 27, 1757
Sunday

Was very dull and lifeless in Duty—Little engagedness of heart in Religion [and] little spirit to pray, and when I did, I felt so hipocritical and formal I cou'd not continue in the duty—O hated Temper—I think I loath my self!

FEBRUARY 28, 1757
Monday

In a sort of Careless Lukewarmness. I am a wonder to My self! How can this be? After such inlightnings, such elivation thus to sink! It teaches me that I am nothing—Had not that opportunity for secret duties as I wanted to have—Read My Monday Portion, but It seem'd a Letter, not Spirit, only when the Spirit giveth it Life.

Eve
I can't be easy with my dead Temper of Mind.

MARCH 1 and 2, 1757
Tuesday and Wednesday

Felt wofully indifferant—Little spiritual mindedness—Was deprived of Opportunities for secret Prayer, and when I catch'd now and then a season, felt dead and drag'd in duty rather from a desire than delight in them. I felt uneasy to find such a temper and that to spend the P.M. in Prayer and began as Usual in which I felt more life than since Sunday and some encouragment to proceed in Duty, but was then prevented by one coming in—'Tis time to enquire what meaneth this withdraw of Life and Light and Spiritual Comfort! Surely God expects me to search this out!— I find no living near to God with out much Prayer and Meditation and strict watching—Otherways Carnality will grow upon me—I think sometimes I had rather endure those terrible Conflicts than this Indifferancy— Conflicts produce Fear, watchfullness, etc., but this is a Monster portion in Many Sins and Desertions—O wretched sinfull heart!

MARCH 3, 1757
Thursday

Still deprived of my wanted retirement, still wofully negligent—Yet I seem to be out of my Element—Can't take comfort in any thing—I think

Nothing but nearness to God is worthy the name of Life. To live as I am now is only Breathing—At Dusk found more life in Secret Prayer—My Spirit seem'd on the Search for God—I sleep but my heart waketh.

Eve
Company was a burden—My Spirit Languishes. I feel as one forsaken.

MARCH 4, 1757
Friday

Remain'd at a distance from God, lifeless and vain—Saw I was far from what I wou'd be and ought to be.

MARCH 5, 1757
Saturday

Deadness cleaves to me—Felt more weary and groned for deliverance—I feel not that delight in Creatures as formerly—So that I seem as one that has neither Comfort in Life nor in any thing Else—I can't take Pleasure in any thing—Whom Have I in heav'n but God, and I think theres nought on Earth I desire in compare with him! Spent part of the P.M. in Prayer for Divine Quicknings that I might run [?] the way of Gods Commandments—Was distress'd with my dead Temper and had more freedom and I hope some Faith in Prayer and was encouraged to hope that I shou'd again have Cause to Praise him for the Light of his Countenance and the Presence of his Grace.

I loath My self in every view I can take and Long to be Sanctified and to live nearer to God—Lord, Pity and help, for thou art my chosen Portion—I renew my choice and beg that I never may retract it, but let me be tyed to thee by a thousand-fold Stronger Obligation—What is there here in this barren Land to solace me? I can't take pleasure in Creatures. I can't take pleasure in My self; 'tis thee, abstractly Thee. O thou Alltogether Lovely One that is worthy my Homage, Love, Choice, pursuit, and Obedience, and Let me have thee, and I will gladly forego all for Thee! I can't take up with less!

MARCH 6, 7, AND 8, 1757
Sunday, Monday, and Tuesday

Felt more engaged in Religion than for some days past. And while I am reading that Excellent Treatise *Owen on Spiritual Mindedness,* I endeavor to bring my heart to a strict Scrutiny, and I do hope I have good ground to judge. God has savingly renewed My Affections and that I am chiefly Concerned to have 'em more and more renewed. Mr Boyse on the *Internal Evidence of Christianity*, confirm[s] me much—I praise my Bountyfull Lord for the Distinguishing helps he affords me (beyond allmost any of my Age and Sex) of Divine knowledge and christian Piety.[66] For such a Father, such Ministers, such a sister [and] such Books as he favoured me with.[67] How can I be Eno' Thankfull!

MARCH 9, 10, AND 11, 1757
Wednesday, Thursday and Friday

My Bodily disorders are of that sort which prevents my justly stating the Temper of my Mind, yet alass! I see I have soul disorders and might take more pains to live to God. I am prevented My Usual seasons for Prayer, and that is disagreeable. O, to have a more constant Spiritual Mind and to live to and on God; I have some relish (tho', ah me, 'tis small) for Divine Objects and christian Duties.

MARCH 12, 1757
Saturday

I have lately been perplexed with a [. . .] case not to be mentioned [. . .]—Yet as God in his Providence has brought it on [. . .] I think it My Duty to [. . .] all on the consideration of it, and I am enabled daily to spread it before the throne of Grace and feel like a weaned child waiting to know the Mind of God and then to act either one way or the other—My Inclinations are more [. . .] for it, but I labor to throw them away and with singleness of heart to Consult Duty only.[68] I feel willing to wait Gods time to have the Path of Duty made Plain to me.

MARCH 14, 15, AND 16, 1757
Monday, Tuesday, and Wednesday

Some gleems of Light begin to apear thro' the dark Clou'd that has so long hung over me, and I feel some degree of trust that God is about to show me the path of Duty—I have freedom to spread and Leave my case with a Covenant God Whose Truth is Engaged for my Security—O, I desire to be entirely subject to him in all things—How sweet is the Peace which flows from a Believing resignation of My All to him.

MARCH 19, 1757
Saturday

Further openings of Providence—But I feel jealous of my decietfull heart least I am not resigned intirely to God. For this I long more than for all Riches.

MARCH 20, 1757, AND DISTRESST OF GOD
Sunday

Last Eve Much Unbelief from whence sprung great dejection and Mallancholly. This Morn Was help'd to go to Christ and beg more holiness, More Faith, [and] More Submission. In Great distress and Mallonchollly Thoughts—Bodily Illness then took Place, and I felt ready to Sink all day.

MARCH 26, 1757
Saturday

Light daily breaks through the cloud, and I am brought to a Satisfaction that [. . .] God in his Providence now calls me [. . .] to consider of it. Difficulties I have to grapple with and at times Unbelief works, and then I either sink or am all in a tumult of anxiety—God help'd me to spend a good part of this P.M. in prayer to him relating to the whole of my Case; I had some Freedom and some Confidence and trust and resignation delivering my whole case into his Gracious Wise hand—O! 'tis sweet to lay over my Burden on him and Wait for his salvation—I never sought nor trusted him in vain, nor I never shall—How very Gracious is he? How Ungratefull, how slow of heart to believe am I?

MARCH 27, 1757
Sunday

'Tis my Earnest desire that I may have the Gracious Presence of God with me [. . .] all my Talents and Opportunities may be wisely and dilligently improved for him—That I may be a Blessing to all about me and that In all Circumstances, Companies, and relations, I may adorn the Doctrine of Christ, be a Pattern to believers and God, be glorified by [. . .]. 'Tis my chief Fear least I dishonour him—I feel calm and have some reliance on him to over rule all for his Glory and my Good—Feel a dependance on him to manage and dispose each menuite Circumstance relative to me [. . .]—My

Christian friends all think 'tis the voice of Providence, and I have seen rea-son to be Astonish'd at the dealings of God to me. Why me, Lord, why me!

MARCH 28, 29, 30, AND 31, 1757
Monday, Tuesday, Wednesday, and Thursday

Met with more sinking trials and was under the prevailing Power of Malloncholly—Cou'd not take hold on a Covenant God But felt unspeakably distress.

APRIL 16, 1757
Saturday

The past fortnight I have been so oppress'd and under the prevailing Power of Malloncholly and Bodily Weakness that I dare not write my thoughts least I make a false judgment but in the Main Cou'd not have any Faith or freedom in holy duties, and now I feel Better in Body but awfully Lukewarm; and God has saw fit to visit me with a sore trial to shake me off my Lees and bring my wandring heart back to him[69]—A person who pretends great Friendship is trying hard to hurt my character and paints me in Black Colors to strangers [. . .]—I know I am vile in heart, but God has not suffered me to practice villany, and the reproaches she throws out against me are Very false.[70] I can appeal to God that they are, and now I desire to commit my Way and Name to him and to trust in him 'till he bring forth my Judgement as the Light and my Righteousness as the Noon day. I have often Experienced his faithfullness in doing it, and why shou'd I distrust him Now—He is as able [and] as full of Grace as Ever he was. O, that I cou'd roll my case over on him who is faithfull and will sustain me.

APRIL 23, 1757
Saturday 13 P.M.

Sat apart this P.M. for very solemn purposes. (O, that I cou'd say with a Solemn Temper) vis to implore the Presence of God on the Morrow at his Holy Table from wherein I have been detained by Bodily Illness ever since January 30, and as I trust [. . .] can answer either Pro or Con to [. . .], given I desire sincerely to seek the Divine Direction, for so far as I know, I wou'd not take a step with out—I dread nothing more than to be left to my own Judgement uninlightened by God.

My stupid heart drag'd heavily, but I dare not deny that God granted me some assistance in spreading my case before him and seeking Grace to help in every time of need—and that he enlarged my views and help'd me to hope for an answer of Peace—Nor can I say I have had more freedom in asking Mercy for Others, My Parents, my little cos(s) [cousins], our servant, My Minister, Church, and Congregation in recommending the New Psalms to him for a Blessing and to be introduced with out Uneasiness into our Church—For the Town, the Land, our Nation, and its dependances—the King, the King of Prussia, all the Protestant States and Nations[71]—Persecuted Protestants in France and for the colledges—for all my dear Friends every where—And for the Indians, Yea, for Jews and Gentiles and the Effusion of the spirit Every where and the happy reign of Christ—I trust it was not in vain that I kept thro' [the] P.M. thus, and I hope thro' the Merits of Christ and his Prevalent Intercession to recieve a Gracious Answer.

APRIL 24, 1757
Sunday

I have this day been to Gods house and Table; I trust had the presence of Christ and some Faith in Exercises and was help'd to renew my Covenant with God and give my all to him and to plead for his Presence and gracious direction in that most important affair now depending—I desire to be Led by him and to have No will distinct from him!

APRIL 30, 1757
Saturday

God has appeared remarkably for me and literally answered my prayer the past Week, to him be all Glory. Still he keeps me at the Foot of his Throne, and O, what an Unspeakably Gracious Condescendion that he allows me to approach it!—In what better way can Mercy Come to a sinner than by a Saviour! I am now waiting to see the final Issue of the affair. Waiting a divine decision, I wou'd not decide it My self for the World. Nothing but a firm perswation of its being aprov'd by God can bear me through it. My Natural inclinations are still [. . .] and I can't alter 'em, but I most earnestly beg that God wou'd encline 'em to that which is most for his honor, let it be which way it will. To him I have entirely left it, and if he changes 'em, I shall see the Whole to be his doing, and it will be Marvellous in my Eyes.

I can never be thankfull eno' for what Ive seen of God in this allready—I can not be thankfull eno' that he more and more deadens me to the Worldly Prospects now in view and that now while the riches of the World are offered me, he helps me to account them mean, base [and] unworthy; my case and love, yea, [lose?] and drop in compare with him!—I have chosen; I again choose God in Christ for my Portion, my Riches, my Inheritance [and] my Highest Good in Time and thro' Eternity.

MAY 6, 7, AND 8, 1757
Friday, Saturday, and Sunday

I'm again in extreem Perplexity—My Inclinations are [. . .] for a Compliance, but what is the main spring that God turns them? I am at a loss to Know—O, how Ignorant of my self. I fear 'tis from a Proud, Ambitous Temper that 'tis a Contrariety to his Will and that I have too much respect to the Cencure of Men and don't regard singly or chiefly the Will, Glory, [and] Providence of God in this Affair. Again I am ready to think I ought to [. . .] and therfore God turns my heart [. . .] and thus I'm tossed about—I can't determine of My self—Not because Friends advise to it—Lord, I am Oppressed. Undertake for me. I will hear no voice but thine; none can direct and lead but thou Alone!

MAY 9 AND 10, 1757
Monday and Tuesday

My thoughts were so fix'd on God that the Applause or Cencure of Mortals was as nothing to me—I saw so much of Gods ruling [and] directing influence, so many Litteral answers to Prayer, so many weighty reasons to move me to comply that I dare not reject tho' I felt loth to accept, upon which I determined to labor to sacrifice my own Will to His, and instantly I felt Ease of Soul.

MAY 11 AND 12, 1757
Wednesday and Thursday

Peace of Mind flowing from a desire to aprove My self to God—From a subjection of soul to Him and a reliance on his Covenant, Faithfullness atended me.

[...] Casting My all for Time and Eternity on My chosen Portion and renewing my Choice of Him for my only Good, I felt a most happy Serenity—I left the Event intierly to him and cou'd say whether Adversity or Prosperity be my lot, still I shall be safe—I left it to him to make just so happy and in that way and time as he pleases; only let me have the God of Gods for mine—His favour, Grace, [and] Presence, and 'tis Enough.

MAY 14, 1757
Saturday Eve

God in Mercy keeps me in Peace; my mind being stayed on him and trusting in him, and why shou'd I fear since the God of salvation is my helper?

MAY 21, 1757
Saturday Eve

My Trials have been great the past week, but underneath were the Everlasting Arms—I am an Astonishment to many and Cencured by many [...], but I see the hand of a Wise God in thus suffering me to fall under the scourge of the Tongue—My support is That God is on my side, I think. [...] he call'd me to think seriously of this change. As [it was] his call, I accepted it and not as my own invention—My Conscience acquits me and if My God aproves, why shou'd I fear the Censure of Worms—All who are acquainted with my true situation think 'Tis a Plain Duty and The Finger of God is seen in it. Adored be his Grace. He gives me all this while such a nearness to him as that my soul despises all Creatures and Creature Enjoyments in compare with him.

MAY 22, 1757
Sunday

This day have renewed my Covenant Engagements to be the Lords and left my Cause and case with him to do therewith what he pleased. Still he grants me to find that he is my Refuge and that the secret of the Lord is with those that fear him; to them does he show his Covenant. O! happy day of Heavenly Grace. I will be the Lords to Obey, serve, and Love him, to seek his Will, and [to] preferr his Glory—Let the World say what they Will!

JUNE 1, 1757
Wednesday

My trials have been great, but all the Bitter Waters have been sweetened by Covenant Love.[72] I have passed thro' a Flood of Cencure, cruel reflections, slander, Calumny, etc. I but have maintained a happy serenity—Yea, been thankfull for it—It has been made a powerfull mean to show me the Vanity of Creatures and the importance of having an Interest in the Favour of the Unchangable God. It has given me a pleasing Evidence to My self that the Aprobation of God was all in all in my Eye; for having that, the Cencure of all the World is nothing to me.

JUNE 5, 1757
Sunday

Still am Undetermin'd what to do and daily meet with Trials of various kind, I am ready to say Woe is me that I sojourn in Mesech and dwell in the Tents of Kedar.[73] I'm sometimes made to Possess Nights of Anguish and days of distress and am on the Point of Sinking; but Everlasting Arms have hithertoo supported, and Everlasting Arms will be the same for the future as they have been for the Past. ("Tomorrows Mercies will be sufficient for Tomorrows Trials," saies Dr Guise).[74] Is not it best to live in a constant dependance on God? Is not it the sweetest way of receiving Mercy, vis by Prayer, faith, hope, [and] Patient Waiting? Did I ever repent waiting Gods time? Have I not allways found his time the Best time? Seen and rejoiced in it? 'Tis true, therefore, I will look to the Lord; I will wait for the God of my salvation; My God Will hear me.

JUNE 19, 1757
Sunday

In the Morning had some desires after God—some pantings after greater degrees of Holiness than Ever I yet attain'd to—Long'd for Universal Holiness in heart and life to Love God more and be more subjected to him than Ever—Saw it to be so Precious as that was probably the greatest Pains I cou'd Possibly take. Went to meeting [and] felt a wandring Mind, but was burdened with it when Behold, Before I was aware my Soul was made as the Chariots of Aminadab![75]—I dread more than any Evil—O Lord, I beseech thee, Get Glory to thy self by all thy dealings with thy nothing Worm, and then I desire to say, here am I; dispose of me Just as thou Pleasest.[76]

64

JULY 2, 1757
Saturday

I seem to be left allmost to [. . .] of [. . .] from my peculiarly [. . .] in this life. I am left [. . .] of [. . .] from [. . .]—and things grow [. . .] and [. . .] I dare not open my whole mind to any Earthly Friend—But still the throne of Grace is Accesible, and there I can and have and do pour out my whole Soul to My Covenant God, my Best Friend, My supream Good; and O, the Divine Pleasure that results from a firm Confidence founded on the truth of his Word and confirmed by *present sensible Experience* that neither tribulation, nor distress, Neither the Frowns of Men, nor the Malice of Divels—nor any thing can separate me from his Love!—I am Upheld by inward support by Everlasting Arms, or sure I am this spirit wou'd fail and this soul sink under her many distresses—The chief Thing on which I Live and from whence my soul derives all her Consolation is that None can rob me of my God; my soul cleaves to him with Unshaken desire and choice; and tho' all the dear Friends on Earth forsake, *yet he will never leave* [and] *never fail me.* 'Tis My Glorious Solace in immence distress.

This has long been my refuge—a refuge that never fail'd—a refuge I've tried and prov'd to be sure in a thousand and ten thousand instances In the near views of Eternity—In the time of the Earthquake and in seasons of Illness when I have been brought to the brink of Death[77]—And now my Soul, thou mayst try it with Safety Again—Now when all other Prospects fail, see to it and let the World see that thou canst Live upon thy God—Evince to thy self [and] Evidence to the World that The Christians Portion [is] in an allsufficient, Ever-abiding, Unchangable Good. Shame to thy self and disgrace will it bring to thy Profession and what is more, displease thy God if thou harborest an Unbelieving, an Anxious, or a dejected Temper of Soul—Burdens thou has too heavy for thee to bear but no cause for sinking, as long as that word stands in thy Bible. *Cast thy Burden on the Lord, and he will sustain thee*; and it will stand there as long as the World stands.

JULY 16, 1757
Saturday

Malloncholly glooms have possess'd me for some days, and I Cant Exercise one grace—can't feel any Life in Religion! Woe is me; I am prone to sin and a sinfull distrust of God! What cause for Self loathing and deep abasement before God at his Holy Table?—It seems impossible I am the same

Creature [as] at Last Sacrament. O, the distance I am now from God!—I wish I was truly humbled at his Feet!

July 17, 1757
Sunday

Partook of the sacrament in the most stupid Manner! I have not had so great a Withdrawment of Life in that Ordinance for years. And yet I feel Easy!—I was thoughtfull whether I had not better stay, but I dare not do so—No Sorrow for sin—No sense of any spiritual things. I have Cause to search narrowly for the Action that has provoked a Holy God to depart from me and to fear a continued withdraw of his Influences from me. O, that I could allways Live near to God!—I don't call it living as I now am! 'Tis only breathing.

August 14, 1757
Sunday

Malloncholly and distress'd. Public and Private affairs Extreamly Dark. And My Soul full of Woe!

August 15, 1757
Monday

Cruel Treatment and Bitter reflections from those who have made great Professions of Friendship and high Boasts of Godliness Make me to cry, O, that I had the Wings of a Dove, etc.[78]—My Mind has been for a Month past the Seat of Distress on my own Account and on Account of the Public Distress, My Dear, Dear Country![79]—But what adds Pungency to my Grief [is that] I feel awfully Unsibmisive to Gods Will!—Cou'd I resign to him, Neither men, nor Divels cou'd hurt me. O, to feel Sin _in me_ the Worst Evil, and the Displeasure of God the heaviest Punishment.

August 22, 1757
Monday

I've taken a new method and I find my account in it vis; when I hear of any Base reflections and any false things Cast on me and meet with Unkind treatment, I cast it on that Promise all things shall work for Good, etc. I then go and tell my Lord of my Injuries and Put him to his Word to make such a thing work for my Good. I Plead for Patience and forbearance and Meekness and Fortitude and a Forgiving temper and beg that the more I recieve of Ill at the hands of Men, the More strong my assurance of his Unchangable Love may grow and that I may Live more Upon him as Better than all Creatures. Then I rise off my knees with Serenity of Soul having lodged my apeal with God, and I find he is to me (in this season of slander) a shadow of a great Rock in a Weary Land. Having [. . .] Period that discordant [. . .] which has been too long [. . .] consideration, I have sat apart this P.M. for secret prayer to beg of God the Help of his Grace to behave suitably under all his Dispensations [and] Grace to see his hand in all.

August 27, 1757
Saturday

What shall I say but "O, the Heights and depths of the Wisdom and Knowledge of God—How unsearchable are his Judgments and his Ways past finding out!—O, for Faith, Humble resignation, and chearfull reliance of Soul on Gods Covenant care—He can Make it work for Good. All things are possible with him.

October 8, 1757
Saturday

God in Holy and Righteous sovereignty has now Touched me in a near and heart-rending stroke, the Death of the most Usefull and Valuable Friend I ever had! (Except my Brother and Sister and Mrs Burr) and at the Juncture when I more needed him than Ever I did. When of all the Friends I have on Earth, he only cou'd do the Special Service (I now Want) for me. But God now shows me that I and all my hopes and Comforts are in his hands—He shows me in a most Evident Manner that the all of Creatures are broken Cisterns that can hold no Water![80]

My Late, Dear, and Firm Friend Mr President Burr Was Possess'd of Every Quallity that is requisite to Friendship.[81] The most generous [and] refined, his character will ever remain inscribed on my heart; as long as I live in this Embittered World shall I continue to Mourn my Loss. But what shall I say. I dare not complain (even in Thought) of God; I see he has done Justly—I see this Rod is pointed at Me, and I own I have deserved it[82]—I can't help adoring the Sovereignty that strikes my Comforts Dead and in one fatal hour has Cast my Prospects into Darkness and Destroyed the Hopes I had been pleasing My self with for 5 years past vis, that in this Dear Man I should find the Brother, the Friend, the Guide, and (If I outliv'd my Father) the Father—Yea, we had intended to Live together.[83] But O! What is human Bliss [but] an empty Shadow—a Night vision! I can't but say 'Tis one of the heaviest strokes I ever met with and the suddeness of it—No warning [and] in full Expectation of seeing him here next Week. O, how Elated I was—never such disapointment—But still selfish as my vile heart is, I mourn more [and] I feel more for the dear Relict than for My self; she lays on my heart Night and day—I have no comfort but in carrying her and her babes to the throne of Grace and Pleading for her all Grace in this time of need—Pleading for them Convenant Mercies That God wou'd be Better to her and Comfort her with his Consolations and support and take Care of her at all times—O, methinks I can pour out my Whole tho' bleeding Soul for them.[84] I trust am helped to wrestle for a Blessing for them and that God wou'd sanctifye it to the Colledge and repair this Great breach and Sanctifye it to his Aged Mother, and to all related and concern'd and acquainted; and O, that I may get more ripened for a Glory by it.

OCTOBER 9, 1757
Sunday

O, my Stupidity scares me! To think I shou'd remain so secure under such a Rod—so impenitent, so Unhumbled—I fear 'tis in Judgement and that I shall misimprove it—This Dispensation is a Loud Call for Deep Self-abasement and Repentance! O! that It might be a means of bringing and of keeping me nearer to God than Ever—My Earthly Comforts are one after another taken away, and if their failure draw'd me to live on God, I shou'd be a gainer—But ah, I fear I grow more rebellious and stubborn under his Correcting hand. Lord, Pardon, Quicken, and Sanctify for thy Dear Sons Sake. Amen and Amen.

NOVEMBER 5, 1757
Saturday

I hope I have had somewhat of the Presence of Christ with me and Some Actings of Soul to him the past month—and some assistance in improving Providences; yet alass, I am at an awfull distance from him—Feel carnal and earthly and too anxious about my Case and stupid to holy Things—Sat apart this P.M. to seek divine Quicknings—to seek the Presence of Christ at his house and Table and the increase of Holiness—more Love and delight in God, more hatred of Sin, and further Mortification, and that I may be brought nearer to God and live a life of holy Devotion to and holy Communion with him—and be more dead to all other Objects whatever—O! that my sacrifices may be Accepted thro' the Great Sacrifice; on that only dare I depend.

Eve

I have been Comemorating My Saviours Dying Love, But ah how little Love to him who Bled and groned and Dyed for me! How stupid—no sensible Communion with him—Yet I felt some acts of reliance on his attonement and some faint desires of Conformity to him and in particular in submission to the Will of God in all things.

NOVEMBER 9, 1757
Wednesday

I feel ready to sink and were it not that I have at times some glimpses of Gods Unchangable Faithfullness, Power, and Mercy, I shou'd utterly despond—But he allows me some freedom at the throne of Grace and to resolve that tho' he slay Me, yet in him I will trust and Look to him for Salvation; and If I perish, it shall be crying and pleading for Mercy in the Name of Christ Whose glorious Name is all my hope—I plead his Acceptable Obedience, Meritorious Sufferings, his Dying Love, and Prevaling Intercession; and I find no hope but in him; the all of Creatures are non-Entit[led]. Spent this Day alone in my Chamber as a day of secret Humilliation and Prayer for to humble my heart Under Gods Mighty hand in Taking my Best Earthly Friend Mr Burr from me—and Under other Frowns of Providence to beg the Pardon of sins past and grace to preserve from sin [and] to assist in right improvement of Providences and More Holness of heart and Life. [I] wrote my secret desires in Devout Miscellanies.

NOVEMBER 12, 1757
Saturday

Some reviving hope that God will draw me nearer to himself by affliction, sweeten the rod by his Love, and deign to Purifye and ripen me for glory by all my distresses of one kind and another, spiritual and Temporal—In this hope is all my Comfort!

DECEMBER 27, 1757
Tuesday

God apeared this day and the past to hear My Cries and give grace to help in time of Need—The throne of Grace has allways been a throne of Great Grace to me—And I never took refuge in it in Vain. God is My Chosen and only Sure Friend—Remember and wait for the Mercies asked of him this Evening.

JANUARY 1, 1758
Sunday

God has led me on to another year. O, that it may be fill'd up for him—I am going to his house and Table, and there I desire to make an Offering, a free will chearfull off'ring, of my all to God—To Accept of his son as my saviour, to Avouch the Lord for my Ruler, My head, my Portion, and Leave all my desires with him—Leave my case as a blank in his hands to be fill'd with what ever he pleases—I desire to go mourning for sin and to roll all my Burdens on him.

Eve
I trust I was help'd to carry all My Load and leave all My Cares with God and leave it to him to do what he pleased with me the Ensuing year.

JANUARY 29, 1758
Sunday

I saw a little, and but a little, of the aversion I have to Holiness [and] My deep-rooted rebellion and opposition to God. I saw a little of My Awfull Pride and self-seeking and that 'twas from hence my heart was so discontented with Divine Allotments—I saw a little of My Carnality and sensuality and that I was far from that Subjection to God that his just and every way Equal Law required—I saw a little of my vile heart and I trust the sight of sin was a true tho' faint one, for it apeared Odious, not only as it deserved and merited Punishment but chiefly because was contrary to that Allegiance which 'tis most suitable I shou'd Pay to My Rightfull Sovereign—'Tis fit, exquisitely fit, that I shou'd seek his Glory, study his

Will, Prefer his Favour, be conformed to his whole Law, and Entirely subject to his Dispose and that I deny My self, my Will and Affections, and Choice and interest when Ever they come in Contrast with his. I trust I felt it an Evil thing and bitter that I was so far from this Temper, that I Carried this Burden of [. . .] to the Lord at his Table and Essay'd to lay it over on him for Pardon and Deliverance from the Power of Sin.

FEBRUARY 25, 1758
Saturday

O, I feel that I want Conformity to God in his Nature by Loving and Delighting in him above all things—by submission and hearty According to his whole will in all that he orders, however Severe—What Contrariety to this resides in this heart! O, 'tis amazing what a Fountain of it remains after all the Pains God has Taken (to speak after the Manner of Men) to subdue me to Himself—I've felt so much of this as has made me afraid to Venture to aproach his holy Presence at his Holy Solemn Ordinance on the Morrow—Yet I dare not refrain—There I wou'd go with My load of Guilt and Enmity and with the Bitter herbs of deep Contrition Comemorate the sufferings of that Loving and Lovely Saviour who died to Procure Pardon and Cleansing, reconciliation and Peace with God, [and] Sanctification and Compleat Redemption[85]—There I wou'd go and Cast My self at his Feet and resolve if I Perish, to Perish there. Let me, O, Divine Redeemer, touch but the Hem of thy Garment, and I shall be made whole of my Plague.[86] Give me a new, a holy Temper to Make me Wholy Subject to Thee, and I shall be happier than If I was sovereign Mistress of the Globe with out it. This is my want, this my Burden, and thou only Canst deliver me. Give me but this and I am Content—O, deny me not this, and I will Seek and Love and Chuse and Preferr and Pursue after thee. O, for a sight of Christ in his superlative Beauty, and it will captivate me; and I shall loose My affections to Creatures in the Flame of Divine Love.

APRIL 21, 1758
Friday

"God will have no Rival in the heart which he sanctifies for himself."

God in Holy but Awfull severity has Again struck at one of My Principle springs of Earthly Comfort. In taking from me the Beloved of my heart, my dearest Friend Mrs Burr—This is the heaviest affliction next to the Death of My dear Sister Mercy I ever met with. My whole Prospects in this World are now changed. My whole dependance for Comfort in this World gone—She was dear to me as the Apple of my Eye—She knew and felt all my Griefs, she laid out herself for my good, and was ever assidously studying it. The God of Nature had furnished her with all that I desir'd in a Friend—Her Natural Powers were Superior to most Women, her knowl-edge was extensive of Men and Things, [and] her Accomplishments fine—Her Prudence, forethought, and Sagacity wonderfull—Her Modesty rare—In Friendly Quallity, none Exceeded her. She was made for a Refin'd Friend. How Faithfull! How sincere? How Open hearted? How Tender, how carefull, how disinterested—And *she was mine!* O, the tenderness which tied our hearts!—O, the Comfort I have Enjoy'd in her for allmost 7 years. O, the Pleasant days and nights we have spent in opening our whole Souls and pouring them into each others breasts! O, the dear Prudent Advice she gave me under all my difficulties—O, the Pleasure of seeing, hearing, loving Writing, Conversing, [and] thinking we took in Each other. O, the Lovely Pattern she set me—The Grace appearing in her Exalted her above all—A bright Example of Personal and Relative, social and Divine Duties—A Dutifull, Affectionate, Respectfull, Obedient, Tender Daughter and Wife. The Tender yet discreet and wife, Mother, and Mistress—The every way loving and lovely Sister and Friend—A Pattern of Meekness, Patience, and Submission under heavy trials—The Mortified, Humble, self denied, lively Christian—Generous, Affable, Courteous, and Kind to all—But—She is gone! Fled this World; forever Tired she longed for rest—Dead to this world. She Prayed and panted and Agonized for a Better, and with her went allmost the *all* in which I had sum'd up my Earthly Good! O, Painfull Seperation! A Desolate world, how Barren art thou *now to me!*—A Land of Darkness and a vale of Tears and no lightsome ray is left me—My Earthly Joy is gone! Not only so, but My God hides his Face! Cant see Love in this dispensation! All seems anger, Yea, Wrath to me! What shall I do? Whether shall I turn? Not to Creatures, for there is none to comfort me! And I do not find Comfort from God—O Wretched Me. God Points his Arrows at me, and I'm ready to say My Way is hid from the Lord; My Judgment is helped over from My God and that he has set me as a Mark for his Arrows!—I'm ready to sink and I can't find my wanted Comfort! O, how shall I drag thro' life—If God supports not, I shall inevitably sink. [A] Great part of my atachment to this World is gone. O! were I ready, I wou'd gladly wellcome the kind summons to follow my dear Beloved into the Valley of Death[87]—Had I the Evidence I want of a title to Glory, Joyfully [I] wou'd quit Earth and all that Earthly minds admire—I want to lay low at the Foot of God and resign to him. I chuse to live at loose from the World and live only on him and have done with Idols and get prepared for Heaven and get more intimate and Pure Acquaintance with Him, the all in all. Lord, Grant these Mercies for thy Sons Sake. Amen.

JUNE 18, 1758
Sunday Morn

My heart is exceeding Backward to spiritual Duties—Full of vain and trifling thoughts, I can't get my Mind fix'd!—O, wretched am I under this Body of sin and Death! When shall I get rid of my sensuality, Earthly Pride, and stupidity. O, to get Purified this day!

AUGUST 13, 1758
Sunday

I have a prospect of waiting on God at his house and Table—But alass! Am not duely prepared—My Mind is vain, stupid, empty of Good, and not Concern'd. Therefore, Feel not the achings of Godly Sorrow, Faith, Love, nor desire after Christ! Scarce Ever felt such a withdraw of Divine Influence as for the past two months—Last Saturday was kept as a day of Prayer with one or two associates in My Chamber, and I thought I found more spiritual Life than for a long while, but I fear 'twas a deception—I don't know how to think it Possible for me to feel so intirely Cold and lifeless in Religious Duties if I was a true Child of God. Lord, I cry to thee to search me and enlighten me and purifye and quicken me to a life of Vigourous Piety, Universal Obediance, and Exemplary Holiness—O, that I might be rous'd from this awfull Lethargy and be earnest for the vital Presence of Christ at his Table this A.M. Awake, O N[orth] Wind, and come thou S[outh] and Powerfully on my soul—with thy Purging and Purifying and Effectual Influences that my Beloved may come into his Garden and Eat his pleasant Fruits[88]—Come, Lord, to the heart that once Lov'd and sought thy Presence!—O, Don't Leave me to hardness, blindness, laziness, and indifferance, to Impenitence and Unbelief, Hipocrisy, and Formallity—Least I be guilty of the Body and blood of the Lord and Eat Judgement to my self!

SEPTEMBER 9, 1758
Saturday Eve

God is again holding his rod over me, and it points at the very Dearest and Best of all my Finite Comforts, the Life of My Dearest Father! Long have I been warned but alass! Am not yet Prepared for the Tremendous Blow— O fatal stupidity!—At times I am allmost sunk with the Prospect and ready to think 'tis impossible to Live under such a Stroke—Can't feel willing—My Views are inexpressibly horrid—I want to be humbled at the Foot of Divine Absolute Sovereignty and Yeild My all to God freely and chearfully as his Due, and for this Temper I wou'd go to his Table tomorrow believing that his Grace is free, full, and allmighty to Effect this and all I need. O, that my Will may be broken and God have the empire of my Will, affections, and whole man intirely. I wou'd deprecate being left of God to hardness, Unbelief, distrust of his Goodness, Impenitency, and unsibmissiveness more than any other Evil I can suffer—O, for Grace to help in this Time of need—all Grace—O, for Meekness and quietness under this heavy trial—O, to be prepared to meet the Holy God in whatever way he may visit me—Correct me, Lord, but with Judgment and in Mercy, or thou wilt bring me to nothing.

OCTOBER 21, 1758
Saturday

Found my Dear Father had entered the valley of the Shadow of Death—O, how heart rending—Cou'd not resign; I was in Unspeakable Anguish all the P.M., Evening and Night—About 8 next morn I went to Bed being so ill [that I] cou'd hold it no longer and never expecting to hear him speak more—I Lay one hour, but no rest of Body or soul had I—I arose in agony—went to him—He could not speak to me—O, how it seem'd!— Surely This is one of Natures tenderest ties, vis the Bond which Unites a Parent and child—especially such a Parent. Never did I experience such Distress as now—I thought when My Sister Died, I felt all that cou'd be felt but [that union] 'twas not Like this Union.[89] Never Was a harder struggle than I felt thro' the day being in such anguish of spirit. A dear Christian Friend came and staid with me all day; and as I cou'd not be composed eno' to bear the Room, we 2 retired and Spent the solemn Day in Prayer For <u>him</u> that God wou'd enlighten the dark valley by his comforting and supporting and inlightning Presence and Make Death Easy and Joyfull and Give a final Victory over Sin and Death, make him perfect in holiness, and

74

transport him to Glory. For the Family that we might Glorify God under this Sore Affliction, be bettered by it, humble, Patient, resigned, and fruitfull. For the Dear Church now like to be bereaved of so able, Painfull, Vigilant, active, Laborious, Faithfull, Wise, a Portion Comitting it into the hands of Christ to be kept from Evill.[90] For his Dear Colleague Pastor that he might be supported and Comforted and helpd under all his Burdens of Labour, Care, and Sorrow.[91]

For Ourselves who share the Part of Children bereaving of their spiritual Father and Pastor—Truly it was the Solemest day I ever Lived. Eternity apeared as Visible—Every spiritual Truth important [and] Death at the door near us. Unspeakably distress'd was I for him and For My self—Satan was suffered to fill me with horrid fears. A Stubbor[n] will raged within. I felt an Enmity rise against God in this his Dispensation But I hope was burdened with it and help'd to wrestle with strong Cries and tears and gronings not to be Uttered for full resignation and Subjection to God; and I felt for about half an hour before he died a wondrous change within. My Will [was] melted and brought to comply, and a happy Calm Ensued. He died in a Gentle Manner at Sunday, October 22.

MARCH 25, 1759
Sunday Two days before marriage[92]

God in his Providence (ever Wise in all he does), having led me to think of changing my state and thro' all the steps leading thereto, having dealt like a tender Father and showing his hand in all, gently dissipating my fears resolving my doubts, and clearing up the Path of Duty, giving me ground to hope a smile of Mercy in this dispensation—And it being near a Completion, I desire this day to humble My self for all my sins Original and Actual of heart and Action—of youth and Riper Age—against God my neibour and My self—and to mourn for all, repent, renounce, and relinquish them with the deepest self abasement—[and to] repair to the Blood and Righteousness of the great Redeemer for Pardon and cleansing and to the Allmighty spirit for Sanctification and with all my heart Unreservedly to give up, Consecrate, and dedicate My self and My all to God to be his and for him his Use. To Love him reign supreamly and Live to him Chiefly, Primarily, and above all—Imploring his Grace, his Presence, and the Blessings of the New Covenant—his Favour and Love in Life, Death, and forever—To Love him, Live to him, be like him, and Enjoy him is all My salvation and My chief desire; and for this I desire to follow him to his Table.

APRIL 15, 1759
Sunday
New Boston

It having pleased God in his sovereign Providence to bring me into a Marriage Union on Mar 27 with one who I Esteem As a Person hopefully Pious and has made me the head of a family—I desire with Gratitude to notice his Goodness herein—that I am placed in Comfortable Circumstances on all Accounts—O, how Bountifull is God to a worthless Worm—I desire and hope I have essay'd to begin with imploring the Blessings of the New Covenant on me, my dear Consort, and whole Family—It has been a great trial that by reason of Lameness I'm deprived from seasons and places of retirement—But God looks to the bent of the heart, and I hope [that] for the merits and Intercession of Christ, my dear Redeemer, [God] will graciously Accept me.⁹³ I desire to renew my actual Dedication to his Service and intreat for Grace to Enable to a due discharge of all the new and various Duties Encumbered on me—I beg to walk beside him in my house with a Proper heart and to set an Example to my Family of Virtue and true Piety. O, for Wisdom from above.

DECEMBER 1759

I have been the Subject of a mixed dispensation since I came to housekeeping [and] have been ridden with Lameness and great pain for some months—With forward, Ungovernable, Ungodly servants, and no small trial is it to see no success of my Endeavour to reclaim them. I trust it has been my sincere desire to have a Family for God—and to have him feared and Served by all in it.⁹⁴ But Alass! God has been awfully suspending [of] the Influences of his spirit from my poor Ser[vants]. At length, after many supplications to him, he has granted me the great Mercy of having a head Servant who is I hope a Pious, Godly Woman; and yet I have the grief to see my younger Servants thoughtless of God, their Souls, their Sins, and Eternity—and tho' I have been crying to him to awaken and give them grace, yet I see no signs of their reformation or of his striving with them— They apear to be hardned in Sin! I am some times discouraged about dealing in secret with 'em, but I am helped still to be faithfull in some measure—But a great burden lays on my heart to see them Graceless, Christless, and going the broad road—I have been sick and very weak for some time, and at times feel as tho' Nature was waning away—These are some of my trials, but the greatest of all is the Unsettled and malloncholy state of the Church I belong Unto—For this I am sore disquieted and for the bigger part dejected—At times I can say I will bear the Indignation at the Lord, but Anon I am full of Uneasy, fearfull apprehensions that God is about to break off Covenant with Us and that a Darker time is coming on this Town and Church than Ever was known since Boston was a Town.[95] O, that my head were Waters and my Eyes Fountain of tears; then wou'd I weep day and night for the dangers We are in of Total Apostasy.

In the Beggining of our dark day, vis Dec 1758—I was assisted with 2 dear associates to spend an Eve every week and some times whole days in Prayer for that dear church. O! What of divine Presence did we happily find eno' to attest to the truth of those animating Words of the Condescending Friend of Sinfull [who] askes, "Where 2 or 3 are met in my Home, there am I in the midst of you."[96] It was our Joint and serious and willing purpose to have continued those social Exercises, But we have been prevented a stated time—Nevertheless we have catch'd at an Opportunity as oft as we cou'd and I hope have been assisted—But What shall I say—An Answer of Peace is not yet given!—God has been sore displeased with Us (as a church). We have left our first love, and he is forsaking of Us! I desire to lay low before him lamenting after him, bemoaning My sins, owning his Justice in the tokens of his Anger, and Our heinous sins as the procuring Cause of all.

JANUARY 6, 1760
Sunday

Now indeed 'tis dark as Midnight and no ray of light appears. It has been my fear for a year past and is now more so than Ever: That God has Wrote an Ichabod on Our church and is avenging the quarrels of his Covenant.[97] I am of the mind more and more that he will feed Us with the Bread of Affliction and not give Us a Pastor as at the First nor a Teacher as at the beginning.[98] If he does, 'twill be "Because We have procured Those things unto ourselves."[99] We chuse our own delusions and reject the sincere, Faithfull, [and] Powerfull Preaching [of] the Gosple of Christ and are still (notwithstanding the most awfull rebukes of his Providence in the affairs of One Mr Potter) hunting after Novelty—Accounting the plain preaching of Christ to be Foolishness panting after Curious Fables and inticeing words of Mans Wisdom—Rejecting plain pointings of Providence and being stricken for what is Call'd at this day Polite Preaching, i.e., as little of Searching, Experimental, [and] vital Godliness as may be—Thus We reject A Man of exemplary Conduct and eminent Grace as well as a Sound Evangellical Divine merely because he is not an Airy Companion nor deals in Speculative and Metaphysicall harrangues.[100]

O, Lord, Pardon, heal, inlighten, and save Us from Utter ruin.

NOVEMBER 2, 1760
Sunday Morn

Yesterday and this Morning I have been endeavouring to look inward and seek to know My case Godward, and I find that I am Evidently under an awfull withdraw of Gracious Influences. The Divine and Holy Agent who us'd to work upon this heart and melt it, who us'd to work on this Understanding and irradiate it, who Us'd to work on this Will and encline it to spiritual Duties and Exercises, [and] who us'd to work on these affections and excite and warm them with the Beauty of Spiritual Objects is now in a great measure departed from me, and [I have] Woefull blindness [and] indifferancy to God—Carnality and Sensual Passions have Gain'd the ascendant; he is just in leaving me, for I forsook him for lying vanities. I can't decipher the Lusts which now prevail nor reckon the number of them; they are many and Exceeding vile! O, my Base Ingratitude, folly, and Sinfullness! How Polluted is my whole Soul!—How vile beyond Compare. I have Cause to fear and tremble when I approach the Holy God—My Perjury, Treachery, and Unfaithfullness in My Holy Covenant—With Low Abasement I desire to approach his holy Presence at his Holy Table this day and with shame and Penitence over my Guilt.

"Against Thee, Thee alone, I've sinn'd
The crime was in Thy sight"[101]

I desire with Self abhorrence to Cast my self at his Feet and beg for a Clean heart and a right spirit—and cry with Davids Temper in Davids Language, Cast me not away from thy Presence nor take thine Holy Spirit from me, but of thine Infinite Grace thro' Christ Pardon, Purifye, and Quicken me, Sanctifye, and Save me from the Power of Sin.[102]

NOVEMBER 15, 1760
Saturday

I have been somewhat stirred up of late to seek after God and his lost Presence—Have had more frequent and spiritual desires after him, been excited to keep some watch over my own heart, and attend more frequently on the duties of Devotion—But ah me! How Cold, how dark, [and] how unaffected is all my Soul. I've reason to fear least God is about to leave me a prey to my own lusts—But O, I dread it more than any Evils. I desire to Cast My self on his Free Sovereign Power and Grace thro' a Redeemer and resolve that if I perish, I will Perish at his Feet—Lord, save me for the Glory of thy Power and Mercy in and thro' Jesus, the allsufficient Saviour of lost Souls.

JUNE 13, 1761
Saturday

After a long season of deadness, Wofull Indifferance, and a Carnal Temper, [I] was brought to some sense of My Vileness and base ingratitude to God and to a determination to seek after his lost Presence, and I cou'd not be easy with out it—Felt *lost* and undone if I had not *God,* tho' I have all things Else—Cou'd and did Justifye him for withdrawing his gracious Influences from me who had acted Contrary to them all—I Earnestly desired and thirsted for his return and his Presence at his Table to-morrow.

JUNE 14, 1761
Sunday

Had a solemn Sabbath, some sence of God, Holyness, and his Grace thro' Christ.

NOVEMBER 8, 1761
Sunday

Still awfully Cold in Religion [and] indulging a Carnal Temper—Taking up with the Form of Duties with out experiencing the Power of Religion— Sometimes I have a short glimpse of the Beauty of real Holiness and near- ness to God. But alass, I am wavering in my desire and remiss in my pur- suits of it. I loath this state! O, when shall I be otherwise! I fear I am a hipocrite.

MAY 16, 1762
Sunday P.M.

I have in the Main for the past Winter been awfully negligent of God— My heart has been Carnal—My thoughts of the Holy <u>God</u> [are] few and slighty—The cares and trifles of Life take up my Time and engross my Mind while God and Christ and my soul are Banished thence—Now and then I seem to awake as out of a dream and am full of shame, self loathing, and sometimes horror. I wonder and am Confounded at my Egregious folly and vileness. I seem to resolve to amend and enter vigourously on a new Course of Living, But ah! My Goodness is transient as the Morning cloud! I return from Confessing Sin to Committing Sin again Untill my Conscience is so defiled that by reason of Guilt and a sense of my reigning Hypocrisie, I have frequently Omitted secret prayer! O, I have taken large strides towards Apostacy!—This day, [this] Month, I was brought to some sense of the Evil and danger of my course and to some desires after renovation, pardoning, and Quickning Grace and did begin work of reformation; Yet I have since that returned as the dog to his vomit again![103] Woe is me!—This day I have been more Engaged to seek for a vital Union to Christ by Faith, for a begun deliverance from the Power of Sin, and a real intire Change of heart Byas and inclination. O, that X wou'd seize me by his Grace and enter into me and possess and rule me by his spirit and his Laws and never let me Wander from him Again.[104] I have had so large Experience of the deciet of my own heart, its weakness, and aptness to go astray that I am afraid to make any more resolutions—Yet I believe I ought to labor to live by some rule and strive that I enter into the strait Gate; and therefore with fear least I forsake my good purposes, I wou'd solemnly beg the help of God in keeping to these following rules of Conduct. So far as health will allow—vis

   I. For the Lords day—Rise Earlier than common, and as Early as possible, Retire to beg Grace to sanctify the Sabbath and ask the Blessing and presence of Christ—Get as much alone for prayer and meditation as possible—Spend as little time in Eating, dressing, etc. as possible.

   II. for Monday
Rise Early to improve the remnants of a Sabbath Frame! Get alone to pray and read a chapter before I go down stairs to my Family—O, the neglect of this has been my ruin!

Ev'ry Following day rise so as to get time for prayer (and if it is possible for reading) before I go down—Order my Worldly affairs so thro' the Week as that Saturdays may not be thronged with Business, and Study to have all the Family work Closed before the Sun be down on that day, that so Servants may be Brought up to venerate and Love the Sabbath—O, Lord, assist me to persevere in the rules and Grant that I may Get and live near to thee forever for the merits [and] sake of Christ on which only I do and I must rely; and if I perish, I perish at his Feet imploring free Mercy.

JUNE 1762

God is visiting Us in this Family with a new and sore Trial, vis in the Delirium of a most valluable Member of it! O, how terrible is God in his Holiness! How does it rise to view when he thus punishes his own *Chosen Ones* (as we have Cause to think her to be). Yet he is Gracious in many respects, Even in this visitation—It might have arisen to higher degrees, even to a total deprivation of reason, and she might have been suffered either to hurt herself or others—Or to speak in the Language of atheism or of profaneness, but God witholds!

JULY 1762

The trial continues and rises to a more disstressing heigth and we know not what to do—God is Holy in all, wise in all, and just in all—He has seen meet also to lay his chastising hand on me in Lameness and thereby renders me Unusefull to others as well as Uncomfortable to my self. But the misery is I do not profit by his Corrections; I neither duely turn to him, nor peneniently Seek his Favour thro' Christ.

AUGUST 16, 1762
Monday

God has encompassed me with Mercy; he has heard and answered Our Cries in *reviving our delirious Servant* and giving in the joyous hope of her restoration, in delivering *another Friend* out [of] hazardous Circumstances, and in restoring me from Lameness. Let this be an Ebenezer.[105]

SEPTEMBER 1762

The Mercy is yet Continued, and we hope Compleating! O, how Good is our God; he is the God of all salvation.

OCTOBER 30, 1762
Saturday

When I take a Survey of My self, my Months, my weeks, and days appear fill'd with Folly, and I fear a decietfull heart has turned me aside and that I have gone so far astray as that It never will be with me as once it seem'd

81

to be. My time has been taken up with the Cares of this World, and I'm prone to make that an Excuse for my neglect of the affairs of my soul when 'tis the Lust within, more than the World with out, which draws me aside. Woe is me for I have Loved Idols and Neglected the Glorious God!—Turned a deaf Ear to the allurements of his Grace and the rebukes of his Rod. Even the love of the Saviour don't affect me; I am hard and Obdurate! I am all over defiled with sin, my Conscience is defiled and hardned, and I am in a worse Case than Ever, [and have] no sense of divine things; they are scarce [and] the Object of my speculative Faith! The Bible seems a dead Letter as to having any Effect on me. I hear sermons [and] I attend Ordinary and Extraordinary means of Grace, but my heart is not in them. All my duties are only shadows, no substance!— What can I think? What can I do? What will become of me!

OCTOBER 31, 1762
Sunday

Roused to some sense of Divine things [and] more engaged in the duties of religion. Had more desires to live to God and to deny My self [and to] take up the cross and follow hard after him—Was more intent in Meditation at the Lords Table than for many months past. Saw where Temptation had Entered and taken hold of me—Saw my neglect of Mortification to the World, its Cares, and vanities; and my Neglect of Secret prayer had been the great Means of bringing me to an Awfull In-differance of spirit in the Business of Religion. Was Excited to Labour against these. At the Lords Table was desirous of bringing these secret Lusts forth and with penitence to seek their Crucifixion—Lord, Let the World be Crucified to me. Let me be Crucified to it, become dead to its snares, deaf to its solicitations, and who ever I offend by this, it preserves me from offending thee. What ever Customs I break thro', Let me not depart from the Way of Duty, which is the way of peace and safety. The Way of Life spiritual Leads to Life Eternal!

NOVEMBER 1, 1762
Monday

I see I have quenched the Holy Spirit and provoked him to withdraw his Enlightning, Exciting, restraining, strengthning, Quickning, [and] alluring Influ[ences] by his Withdraw. I find my Corruptions have gathered

82

Strength—I'm formal and slighty in Duty—Unwatchfull, Unfruitfull, [and] Carnal in my Ends—Unprofitable and Unexemplary to others—I Greatly Displease and dishonour the Holy God—and am (Unless Mighty Grace prevents) in Awfull Hazzard of Apostacy. I desire to seek his return, to Labour heartily, to repent, and turn to him with all my heart and now to shake hands with all Idols, and from this time to be for him intirely. I heard yesterday a sermon Adapted to me from Prov. 4:23.[106] O, that I might be excited [and] as Exhorted *to make religion My Business* and give the World no room in my heart any farther than God allows and requires—O! The World is an Enemy to souls. Christ Overcame it; by him may I also Overcome it, and the Glory of the Grace shall be his alone. For the Strength must, I am certain, be derived from him, or Else the Combat will be Unequal, and the Conquest Never be Won.

As one means of regaining a seriousness of Spirit, I propose to retire Ev'ry night at Dusk for Prayer.

NOVEMBER 8, 1762
Saturday

I think I've been more afraid of sin and more serious in Religious duties the past week and have been desirous and Endeavouring to keep from mine Iniquity [and] from passion over *worldly carefullness*, the Bain of Godliness. But alass, my heart is Cold and treacherous and prone to Backslide. I see where my Weakness lays; may God Enable me to watch against temptation, and to Keep my heart dilligently—O, for a revising of religion in my soul!

NOVEMBER 28, 1762
Sunday

I hope God was nearer to me this day than for a long Season. He has been moving on the Face of the Waters, yea, stirring up the waters of the Sanctuary for my healing.[107] He enabled me to Cry for a suitable Word, and he sent me a Word in season from Rev. 2:4, 5. I hope I had some outgoings of Soul to him at his Table [and] that Christ appeared precious and his Blood sufficient to cleanse and heal me. I Essay'd to devote my self to him, but past Experiences of my treachery made me afraid to depend on my own power to keep my Engagement one hour!

I hope I had a precious day.

DECEMBER 3, 1762
Friday

I trust God has not forsaken me! Tho' I have awfully forsaken him, yet he is Calling after me still—I hope he is near to me in Duty and is drawing me with the Cords of a Man and the Bands of Love that his Truths are more precious.[108] I see a Divine Beauty in his Word and ordinances, and I am restless 'till I get near to him and hold Communion with him.

DECEMBER 25, 1762
Saturday

I trust I have had more real delights in the things of God this past Month and more solid pleasure than Ever I took in the World and all its Gay Allurements. The Word and the divine truths of the Gospel have been prised and delighted in, Especially those which relate to the Divine Person['s] Wondrous office's and the Gracious Actions, Benefits, Love, and Grace of the Blessed Redeemer—I have loved to read of him and meditate on him, yet Alass I know not what to think of my self. My heart is so apt to loose this Gust, to forget this Savour of his Name, to return to sloth, and yet farther to Wander from; and some days I have such a Backwardness to secret Prayer that it is when performed, done, and gone about as a task, and I have no spiritual views of God or desires after spiritual Mercies—Again I get some faint glimpse and seem to Want to have the Enjoyment of Gods Presence and to be fresh brought near to Him, Even to his Seat to Behold his Glory, to see his Beauty and that I may have the highest Esteem of him and Ardent Love to him and heart satisfying Communion with him— Again I return to a dull Indifferance, yea, to an Absolute *Negligence* of him So that I can come to no clear satisfactory Conclusion about my state. If I am a Believer, I'm the Lowest of all. If a Hipocrite, a self decieved one and in Awfull danger of perishing. Lord Jesus, I beg Thee to have pity on me and save me to the Uttermost. Thou canst do it; I believe thou Canst, and I beg thy Free Mercy. True, I am a Great Sinner, but my sins, tho' they deserve Infinite Punishment, do not Surpass thy Powerfull Grace, for that is Infinite—I wou'd Flee to thee and venture on thy Rich Grace, venture my Soul upon thy Grace, and beg to be saved from my Sinfull Nature as well as Guilty state; for the one is my Malady as well as the other! Lord, seize my whole soul, sanctify and Cleanse Every Power of it and let me from this Evening be thine in an Everlasting Union and sure Covenant and never more be my own or the Worlds, but Love, Fear, serve, and delight in thee

Forever.[109] Lord, Let this be the happy Event that shall succeed all my Folly, Vileness, and guilt, the Great Issue of all my Wandrings, my Apostacies, and Perplexities; and thine shall be the Glory forever. Amen and Amen.

DECEMBER 26, 1762
Sunday

I attended the Holy Supper with desire after Christ, and methought I had a refreshing Season and was excited to more constancy and vigour in Religion than for some time past, which temper seem'd to remain for some time.

JANUARY 22, 1763
Saturday

But now, January 22, I am constrained to renew my confession that to do good I am unapt, that I have renewed my Guilt—Have grown vain and carnal in my Temper, and gone far off from God! I am full of Guilt and Impenitence—Hardness and relentess fear seized on me, and I have no real proper Sense of Sin or of my Mallady, nor little desire after the only Physitian!

Eve

I humbly hope the Good Spirit of Grace wrought in me some relentings for sin and that I lamented it sincerely. My Ingratfull Temper (to such a God, such a Redeemer who has been, as it were, wooing me for himself notwithstanding my vileness) apeared as Black as horrid to me; and I cou'd not but abhor my self as a Monster, a very Prodigy of Sin and Guilt.

JANUARY 23, 1763
Sunday

I saw somewhat of my pollution, Guilt, and vileness and cou'd not but loath my self and long for purification from the Blood of Christ. I earnestly Beg'd for this, and with my soul I followed after Christ for it. With desire I went to his house and Table, and methought I wanted to lay ever in the Dust mourning my Sinfull heart and cou'd not be Pacified with any repentance or Exercise of Sorrow—I cried for pardon, but Pardon with out Purity and Holiness wou'd not Satisfy me. I repaired to the Blood of Christ hoping for the Efficacy and virtue of it and Essay'd to give my self quite to

Him to be ruled, Governed, possess'd, and Led by him—I trust I had his Quickning presence with me and that the relish of it still remains.

JANUARY 27, 1763
Thursday

[No entry]

August 6, 1763
Saturday Eve

I've cause to fear and tremble at the prospect of being an Unworthy Guest at Christs Table—Sin prevails—Its power grows; the World has got into if not reigns in my heart—Ah me, I am unmindfull of the Glorious God, a slighter of the Only Saviour!—I have loved Idols and after them I have gone a Whoring.[110] Is there hope for me? Is it not a gone case? Is Christ ready notwithstanding all this to be reconciled? Will he yet mulltiply to Pardon?— Yet he is Willing if I am Willing to forsake all for him, to take up his Cross, and follow him in sincerity. I'll try to Cast this filthy, this Guilty, Lost, per- ishing soul on his Free Mercy [and] his Infinite Grace.

AUGUST 30, 1763
Tuesday

Excited to some seriousness and attention to the affairs of Salvation by the Awfull Providence of God in the Surprising Death of our Junior Pastor, the Rev'd Mr A. Cumming.[111] Eternity apear'd real; Death, certain; Life, short and a vapour. I thought The World appeared an airy Bubble, and I felt desirous to get above it. For some days this Frame Continued.

OCTOBER 2, 1763
Sunday

Felt hardned and Stupid at the Lords Table—My Mind crowded with vain Thoughts. I find the World has gain'd an Awfull ascendancy over me!

OCTOBER 3, 1763
Monday

From a Certain Knowledge that I'm in a deplorable Case, That Sin prevails, The World Enslaves, and my heart is buried in the mire of Sensual pursuits—The Holy spirit is provoked and has withdrawn his Influences from me so that I have no delight in Secret Duties of Piety—Yea, often Neglect them, and my Time and Thoughts are chiefly bent on Worldly Cares and pleasur[e]. I say on a serious view of my Case, I think I am call'd to set apart a Day for secret Humilliation and prayer to search out and confess and bewail my sins and supplicate for Pardon, cleansing, and healing of my woful Backsliding; by Gods leave I devote the Morrow for that purpose (I having so ordered My Family affairs [. . .] I think I can attend it with out the Neglect of other Duties.) 'Tis time to rouse out of my Lethargy. Awake, O sleepy soul, Arise, [and] Call upon thy God. It may be he will appear to my help, or I perish, I perish in my Sins.

> "To starve with hunger here I pine
> I die in foreingn Lands
> My Fathers House has rich Supplies
> And Bounteous are his hands."[112]

I'm starving indeed, but there is a full supply in Christ for every Needy Sinner—I'm an Infinite sinner 'Tis True—But he came to save such— None ever needed him more than I—I'll go and seek him; if I perish, I'll perish there!

OCTOBER 4, 1763
Tuesday Eve

This day was spent as designed in the Following Method:

1st with prayer for assistance
Then sang 1st part of Ps. 139.
Then I endeavoured to Examine and find out my sins.
Then Spread my Case before God—Confess'd my sins and implored pardoning, cleansing, and sanctifying mercy for the sake of Christ—Was straitned in prayer.
Then read Jer. 2 and 3 and a part of a sermon of My Fathers on Jer. 3:12.

P.M.—sang part of Ps. 51.
Then confess'd and made supplication for cleansing and healing and the return of Gods Holy Spirit—Was more enlarged.
Read My Fathers Sermon of Jer. 50:4, 5.
Sang part of Ps. 43 and Ps. 84.
Read Hos. 2.

Then pray'd and spread my spiritual Mallady before God with more Freedom than before [and] beg'd a remedy for each in particular, was more enlarged—Made Intercession For Every Branch in the Family in particular and Spread their Case before God—for Friends and relations—for Our Church and *Dear Pastor*, the other churches and pastors in Town, for the town in General, The Land, its churches, Ministers, Magistrates, Nation, Protestant Church—for the Progress of Christianity thro' the World—for the Indians in North America—the down Fall of anti X and the Flourishing of Xs kingdom thro' the Whole World.[113]

Was help'd to Some Sincerity. I hope 'twas not wholly Formal, tho' alass, too much. I Look to the Blood of attonement for pardon, cleansing, Acceptance, and a Gracious Answer and Can't but have some hope God will grant it. I look'd to God for direction to make *proper resolutions* and at Length came to this: *to spend a Day in this Way as often as* [. . .] *my Family duties will allow.*

Remember the Vows of God and Covenant Bonds. I Entered into this day to be the Lords—O, to keep a Strict watch over my heart is necessary if I wou'd be a Christian Indeed.

OCTOBER 9, 1763
Sunday

I did resolve to be on my Guard this holy day and did hope to Enjoy a day with God, but alass, the motions of the Flesh have been powerfull. I find that a Law in my members warrs against the Law in my Mind [and] that these are Contrary. Whether a Gracious or only a Consciencious Contrary is Uncertain to me—But O my Soul, there is one who knows and whose Judgement is according to the Truth.

JANUARY 24, 1764
Saturday

I find my self at an Utter Uncertainty about my spiritual state. I have been so vain and Carnal in my Temper, so Negligent of my soul, and inattentive to all spiritual objects that it looks dark and awfull. I feel stupid and impenitent and know not what to think of My self—Nor what to do but make an Essay to Look by Faith to him whom God has set forth to be a Propitiation, whose Blood cleanseth from all sin—Never was a viler Sinner; never One needed a Great Saviour more than I do—My Guilt stares me in the

Face when I think of casting My self on Christ. What when I have trampled on him? Crucified him so often over and over again? But I must perish if I don't take this course. If I do, who knows but [that] he will make me a trophy of his Grace. He is able, yea willing, to Save the chief of sinners, and Chief of Sinners is my true Character!

FEBRUARY 12, 1764
Sunday

I know not what Judgement yet to pass on my state. My spots seem of a worse kind than what can stain the true Xn and yet there have been so many Exercises of my mind like Faith in God the Redeemer, like supream love to Him, like delight in Him and cleaving to him [and] pressing after him, like desires and labour and striving to subdue lusts [and] get self dethroned and Christ advanced in me and Holiness take place.[114] That 'Tis a very perplexing case I'm in—I know this: that sin now bears vile in me, the World possesses me, and I am Negligent of God—Don't Love secret prayer, spiritual Meditations, nor close examinations into my self. I had last Night and today some desires to get Acquainted with God, to return to him and take up my rest only in him, but I fear it is only a fleeting passion and will soon vanish away. O, that he Wou'd put forth his Mighty power and draw and bind me to himself. Lord, seize me for thyself and never let me Wander from thee!

MARCH 9, 1764
Thursday

My affairs being so ordered, I have purposed to set apart this day for Secret humilliation and Prayer:

> 1st on account of my own Soul, which is in an Awfull state of distance and disafection to God and his Ways, to seek his Gracious Influences to make me holy; to empty me of Sin, the World, sensual Aims, Corrupt affections and determine me for, and fix me on himself, so as that I may be for him and his Service intirely and forever.
>
> 2cdly for those young ones who are to go thro' the Small pox in my house, to Commit them to God to be kept and carried thro' this Sickness Gently and favourably, for with out him Means are of no Efficacy.

3 for the *whole Town* under his present correcting hand by that Distemper.

4 for *our church*, now vacant, that God wou'd appear to build up our Zion and give us a pastor after his own heart and overule all our Spirits and Corrupt desires and keep us United in his Fear.

And 5th for a *revival of vital Religion* in the Town and Land.

O, I am dead and Stupid and need divine aids to perform the duty of this day. Or I shall prevaricate with God and provoke his Wrath and just displeasure! I desire to depend on him, for he is able to help mine Infirmities!

Eve

I hope I had some sincere breathings after God that wou'd subdue me to himself, rule, and posses me wholly. Some out goings of soul to wrastle for Spiritual Blessings for my self, for those who are committed to my Care [and] For Our Dear Church and Pastor—[for] The Town in this Dark Day and the Land—I am a vile wretch, but I need a Saviour to deliver me from Sin; and I must Continue to Seek and press after him. I hope (tho' I had many interuptions from within and from with out), yet I hope it was not in vain that I sought the Lord this day—And I propose to set apart part of a day this Week and part of a day the next for the same purposes if God give leave. O, that my roving heart may now at last fix on and for God.

My spirit was impressed with a sense of Gods Corrective dispensation to this Town; I think it a day of Divine Rebuke. I saw God was just and holy in thus afflicting Us; I saw a need of being reconciled to him thro' Christ; I hope I was Earnest for this for My self and Family and Town. I saw a need of his Mercy for my Young Folks. I endeavoured to carry them in prayer and Faith to Jesus. I saw he was able to save 'em; and Unless he Undertook for them, Physicans and Means were of no vallue. I saw his Blessing was all in all. I beg'd that our Family might be sprinkled with the Blood of the atoneing Sacrafice, and then I saw all wou'd be well. I gave the children away to God and resign'd 'em over to him and was free to leave them there at the Foot of Mercy, and here my heart got Eased of that distress I had been weighed with, and I felt very satisfied in Gods requirements that in the way of humble hope and free resignation, we shou'd wait for his Salvation. I thought it worthy of him to keep his Nothing Creatures in intire dependance on him for every thing—My heart was in a Measure resolved to trust on him, and I felt no Anxiety about any thing—And now I wait for an answer of Peace!

90

APRIL 18, 1764
Wednesday

God has been Exceeding Gracious to Us in carrying 5 in our Family very Gently thro' the Small Pox so that they are all alive and recovered to health— O, what shall we render? 'Tis a new Obligation on them to Seek and Serve him, and on me to train up those 2 of them Under my care for him, and a new Encouragement to call on and console in him as long as I live.

JUNE 9, 1764
Saturday

This week I have parted with My Dear Friend Mr Whitefield who has been for some Weeks in Town and whose Powerfull Ministry in Public and animating Conversation in Private has, I humbly hope, been blessed of God to rouse me out of my spiritual lethargy and quicken me to remember whence I am fallen and repent and Seek after God.

JUNE 10, 1764
Sunday

My Soul's desire this Morning is to See the Glory of Christ and his Wondrous Love to Man in his house and to take it at his Table. What can I ever expect from a God? He warrants my boldest Expectations—He saith, open thy mouth wide and I will Sanctifye thee![115] Amasing Encouragement.

P.M.

I hope I had real desires after God this Morning—His presence and grace, and that in Secret duties I found it good to draw near him. I wanted to be nearer and nearer and earnestly thirsted for Believing views of his Glory in Christ and for the assimalating Efficacy of such views Transforming my whole Soul into his likeness.

I hope The Word preached was sweet unto me; tho' I was Unwatchfull and Wandring, yet I bemoned my sad state and endeavored to bring my wretched, roving mind to Christ, to who only can keep it from departing from him, My Life.

At the Lords Table I was refresh'd [and] his Fruit was Sweet to my Taste—I desired to give my self wholly to him to be *taught*, *governed*, and *saved* by him. I was Jealous least I was not entirely free and willing to give up every thing for him—To take up his Cross and follow him closely and strictly. But so far as I know my heart, that heart I gave wholly to him and bid him a Glad Well come as my Lord to Obey, as my attoning priest, and enlightning Prophet, and desired to be more strongly bound and more entirely subject to him, my God, my all, than ever before—Thus have I some hope that God in Rich Love will reduce my Wretched Wandring heart to himself after more than Four Years departing farther and farther from him! O, who can conceive how low I have been Sunk in the horrible pit and miry Clay—How empty, vain, and trifling I have been—'Tis Amazing Patience like a God that has bore with my horrid neglect of him. I wonder he has not 'ere this time made me a Magor Messabib and set me up as a warning, a Mark to all apostatising proffesors of his Religion.[116] I fear my heart—I can not keep it; I can't trust it one Moment. Lord Jesus, I fly to thee to keep me by thy allmighty Power thro' faith unto Salvation, or I shall be a cast away—If left to My self, I know I shall fall; but I will depend on thy strength, my adorable head. O, keep me this Week near to thee— Let no sceenes, no Friends, no trials, nothing draw me away from thee!

JUNE 17, 1764
Sunday

God has returned me to my house. Last Saturday I was earnest for the presence of God on the approaching day and Ordinance of the Holy Supper—Was helped to enlargement in Secret prayer and in Contemplations on the deep abasement and Dreadfull Sufferings of the Son of God. Spent the P.M. in Social prayer and religious Conference with —— and —— and retired at Dusk with Sweet Composure of heart to Meditate, pray, and praise. Every incident was a burden that prevented My Soul from fixing itself on God. I arose Early on the Lords day and was Glad at heart it was a Day set apart to Him. I retir'd for an hour and half, and I hope was sincere in seeking him whom I trust my Soul Loveth.

I went with [expec]tation to his house and Table and was not disapointed; he appeared Lovely in Suffering; in dying he appear'd all in all to me, and I gave My all to Him.

Notes

Note to the Reader

1. Sue Lane McCulley, interview with Stuart Walker, Boston Public Library, December 20, 2000.

Introduction

1. Patricia Caldwell, *The Puritan Conversion Narrative: The Beginnings of American Expression* (Cambridge: Cambridge UP, 1983), 41 and 55–6.

2. Sereno Edwards Dwight, preface to Sarah Pierpont Edwards's narrative in *The Life of President Edwards,* in *The Works of President Edwards, with a Memoir of His Life,* vol. 1, ed. Sereno Edwards Dwight (New York, 1830), 171.

3. Jonathan Edwards, "On Sarah Pierpont" in *The Works of Jonathan Edwards,* 22 vols. to date, general eds. Perry Miller, John E. Smith, Harry S. Stout (New Haven: Yale UP, 1957–), 16:789. *Works* will be cited simply by volume number and page. Elisabeth D. Dodds, *Marriage to a Difficult Man: The "Uncommon Union" of Jonathan and Sarah Edwards* (Philadelphia: Westminster P, 1972), is the only full-length biography of Sarah Pierpont Edwards and was enormously helpful in preparing this material, as were the Marsden, Miller, Murray, and Winslow biographies of Jonathan Edwards. See George M. Marsden, *Jonathan Edwards: A Life* (New Haven and London: Yale UP, 2003); Perry Miller, *Jonathan Edwards* (New York: William Sloan, 1949); Iain H. Murray, *Jonathan Edwards: A New Biography* (Carlisle, PA: Banner of Truth Trust, 1988); Patricia Tracy, *Jonathan Edwards, Pastor: Religion and Society in Eighteenth-Century Northampton* (New York: Hill and Wang, 1980); and Ola Elizabeth Winslow, *Jonathan Edwards, 1703–1758* (New York: Macmillan, 1940).

4. William Ames, *The Marrow of Theology* (1629), ed. and trans. John D. Eusden (Grand Rapids, MI: Baker Books, 1968), 80. For a concise and insightful analysis of Edwards's understanding of the role of the affections in religious experience, see Stephen R. Yarbrough and John C. Adams, *Delightful Conviction: Jonathan Edwards and the Rhetoric of Conversion* (Westport, CN, and London: Greenwood P, 1993), especially 5–21 and 28–40. Yarbrough and Adams identified the passages in Ames as Edwards's foundational documents in his "heart religion."

5. See especially *Treatise on Religious Affections* in *Works,* 2:96–118.

6. Qtd. in Marsden, 349, and 572n16.

7. See Sandra M. Gustafson, "Jonathan Edwards and the Reconstruction of 'Feminine' Speech" in *American Literary History* 6 (Summer 1994): 185–212, in which she argues that Jonathan Edwards's late literary style responds to the strength and tenor of his wife's voice in her 1742 narrative. Julie Ellison has examined Jonathan Edwards's use of his wife's document for his ministerial goals in "The Sociology of 'Holy Indifference': Sarah Edwards' Narrative" in *American Literature*

56 (December 1984): 479–95. In "Jonathan Edwards and Sarah Pierpont" in *Foundations of Religious Literacy*, ed. John V. Apczynski: (Chico, CA: Scholars P, 1983), 107–26, William M. Shea attributes the language of Edwards's *Personal Narrative* to his wife's 1742 experience of conversion and the language she invokes to communicate her experience.

8. See Samuel Hopkins, appendix 2, "Containing a Short Sketch of Mrs. Edwards's Life and Character," in *The Life and Character of the Late Reverend Mr. Jonathan Edwards* (Boston, 1852), 113. Rev. Samuel Hopkins of Great Barrington, Massachusetts, was an exceptionally close friend of the Edwards family. Once a student of Jonathan Edwards, Hopkins became a highly regarded theologian and Edwards's ministerial colleague and would later serve as Edwards's literary executor and first biographer. See Marsden, 249–52.

9. Hopkins, 92–98.

10. George Whitefield, *George Whitefield's Journals* (Edinburgh: Banner of Truth Trust, 1960), October 19, 1740, 477. George Whitefield, an ordained Anglican minister and reformed evangelist, was among the most prominent and sensational orators of the Great Awakening. George Whitefield preached from the Philadelphia area to Savannah in 1739 and returned to the colonies in 1740 and 1745 to preach in New York and New England, where he addressed crowds of thousands. Jonathan Edwards invited Whitefield to Northampton and received him in October 1740 and July 1745; while there he offered public sermons and private talks at the Edwards's home. See *Works*, 16:79–81, 174–79, and Marsden, 202–16.

11. Historians and literary critics currently understand that the revival movement signaled by the term "the Great Awakening" had neither the cohesion nor the religious, social, or political importance that was once ascribed to the movement. Jonathan Edwards, who spoke of a "general awakening," a "remarkable season," and a "flourishing of religion," never used the phrase "the Great Awakening," a term attributed to a nineteenth-century work, Joseph Tracy's *The Great Awakening: A History of the Revival of Religion in the Time of Edwards and Whitefield* (Boston, 1842). The shift in scholarly understanding of the revival movement is credited to Jon Butler, whose interrogation of the historical thought on this period concludes, "The label 'the Great Awakening' distorts the extent, nature, and cohesion of the revivals that did exist in the eighteenth-century colonies, encourages unwarranted claims for their effects on colonial society, and exaggerates their influence on the coming and character of the American Revolution." See "Enthusiasm Described and Decried: The Great Awakening as Interpretive Fiction," *Journal of American History* 69.2 (1982): 308. See also Joseph Conforti, "The Invention of the Great Awakening, 1795–1842," *Early American Literature* 26.2 (1991): 99–118. However, this is not to minimize the important and revolutionary work of Jonathan Edwards in the history of Calvinist theology and religious practice and in the history of American letters. Joseph Conforti makes this very point in his elegant study of the role of Jonathan Edwards in the Second Great Awakening of the late eighteenth and early nineteenth centuries, *Jonathan Edwards, Religious Tradition, and American Culture* (Chapel Hill and London: U North Carolina P, 1995).

12. *Works*, 16:789.

13. *Works*, 4:331–47.

14. Sarah Pierpont Edwards, "On Tuesday night, Jan. 19, 1742" in *The Life of President Edwards*, 171–86. Dwight, the editor of this important collection, is the son of Timothy and Mary Edwards Dwight and the grandson of Sarah Pierpont Edwards.

15. Edwards expresses his thoughts on the requirements for church membership in *Treatise on Religious Affections* in *Works* 2:413–20.

16. The decisions of 1657 and 1662 concerning the halfway covenant are found in Williston Walker, *The Creeds and Platforms of Congregationalism* (Philadelphia: Pilgrim P, 1960), 291–339. See also Ames, who states, "The children of those believers who are in the church are to be counted with the believers as members of the church" (179). Edwards expressed his objection to the halfway covenant in *An Humble Inquiry into the Rules of the Word of God Concerning the Qualifications Requisite to a Compleat Standing and Full Communion in the Visible Christian Church* in *Works* 12:165–348 and *Misrepresentation Corrected, and Truth Vindicated* in *Works* 12:349–503, the former originally published in 1749 and the latter in 1752.

17. See his March 21, 1731, sermon, *Self-Examination and the Lord's Supper*, in *Works*, 17: 270–71, and Jonathan Edwards's account of his dispute with his congregation on this subject in "Narrative of Communion Controversy" in *Works*, 12:507–619.

18. See, for example, his December 1741 sermon, "The Curse of Meroz," in *Works*, 22:492–508.

19. "To the Reverend Thomas Foxcroft," in *Works*, 16:323.

20. "To Gentlemen," November 1744 in *Works*, 16:149.

21. Marsden, 301–2, and Patricia Tracy, 158.

22. Esther Edwards Burr, *The Journal of Esther Edwards Burr, 1754–1757*, ed. Carol F. Karlsen and Laurie Crumpacker (New Haven and London: Yale UP, 1984), 135.

23. Burr, 301.

24. Thanks are owed to Sue Lane McCulley, *From the Rhetoric of Ramus to the Rhetoric of the Revolution* (Ph.D. diss., U of Houston, 2002) for information on the biography of Sarah Prince Gill. See especially 7–10. Elisabeth Dodds's biography of Sarah Edwards, *Marriage to a Difficult Man*, also provided important details on the personal relationship between the Edwards and Prince families (61–62). Marsden, Miller, and Winslow offer full and important material on the professional relationship of Jonathan Edwards and Thomas Prince.

25. "The Spiritual Narrative of Sarah Prince Gill," 58. Quotations from the spiritual narratives of Sarah Pierpont Edwards and Sarah Prince Gill are from this collection and will be cited parenthetically by page number.

26. John White, *New England's Lamentations: Under Three Heads, the Decay of the Power of Godliness; The Danger of Arminian Principles; The Declining State of our Church Order, Government, and Discipline* (Boston, 1734).

27. See Burr, 206, for example.

28. Ibid., 53.

29. Ibid., 280.

30. Our understanding of the forms and use of the conversion narrative in seventeenth- and eighteenth-century New England is based largely on four important works: Patricia Caldwell's analysis of seventeenth-century English and New English narratives, *The Puritan Conversion Narrative: The Beginnings of American Expression*; Charles E. Hambrick-Stowe, *The Practice of Piety: Puritan Devotional Disciplines in Seventeenth Century*

New England (Chapel Hill and London: U North Carolina P, 1986), which was helpful in developing an understanding of the function of the conversion narrative within Puritan religious practice; Daniel B. Shea, *Spiritual Autobiography in Early America* (Princeton: Princeton UP, 1968), which studies the varieties of religious expressions of self in the Puritan and Quaker tradition; and most recently Rodger Payne, *The Self and the Sacred: Conversion and Autobiography in Early American Protestantism* (Knoxville: U of Tennessee P, 1998), which focuses on the rhetoric of conversion. In addition, Edmund S. Morgan, *Visible Saints: The History of a Puritan Idea* (Ithaca and London: Cornell UP, 1963), a seminal work, was early to identify the morphology of conversion expressed in the conversion narrative and provides a historical context to the institution of the requirement of the conversion narrative for church membership in New England.

31. See Walker, 223.
32. Thomas Shepard. *The Parable of the Ten Virgins* (London, 1660), 2:200.
33. Ames, 161.
34. See Ames, 168–71 for a fuller explication of sanctification. The morphology of conversion is clearly articulated by John Cotton in *The Way of the Churches of Christ in New-England* (London, 1645), 55. See also Caldwell's understanding of the process of regeneration, 65.
35. Hambrick-Stowe, 199.
36. Note that seventeenth and early-eighteenth-century women's conversion narratives, much like many women's captivity narratives in this period, were regularly mediated by the minister. That is, the minister transcribed and thus authored the female penitent's oral account of her conversion experience and presented it to the church membership. In this way the male voice is superimposed upon female experience.
37. See *A faithful narrative of the surprising work of God in the conversion of many hundred souls in Northampton* in *Works*, 4:176.
38. Payne credits Jonathan Edwards with reviving the use of oral relations within the evangelical tradition and writes that "Edwards stands as the great mediating figure between Puritanism and evangelicalism" with his explorations of conversion and the "religious affections" (23). See also 95n15.
39. Ibid., 11.
40. In this narrative Sarah Edwards makes note of her "First closing with the Lord Jesus," which was her first experience of regeneration (1, 12).
41. See especially Jonathan Edward's *Some Thoughts Concerning the Present Revival of Religion* and *A Treatise on Religious Affections*.
42. Rodger Payne noted this rhetorical feature of conversion narratives in his comments at the Providence meeting of the Society of Early Americanists, March 2003. See also Caldwell, 140.
43. Daniel B. Shea notes that the claim of inarticulateness is "more than familiar; it is . . . conventional in the literature of spiritual experience" (98). See also Caldwell 90–91.
44. Isaac Watts was a Calvinist theologian and London minister as well as an eminent lyricist. His hymns were popular in the colonies and were reprinted frequently. Watts corresponded with Jonathan Edwards and sponsored the London publication of his *Faithful Narrative*. See *Works*, 16:48, and Marsden, 143–44, 171–73.

The works of Elizabeth Singer Rowe (1674–1737), an English religious poet and essayist, remained in continuous publication many years after her death and served evangelical Christians as inspiration for meditation and as a model for their own writing.

As evidence of the popularity of these authors in conservative Protestant circles in New England, Esther Edwards Burr penned a light-hearted comment to Sarah Prince Gill, musing "I wish [Mrs. Rowe] and Doct Watts had got togather and had one Child {so} that {we} might see what they could do" (Burr, 80).

45. Song 24 in John Mason, *Spiritual Songs; or, Songs of Praise with Penitential Cries to Almighty God* (Boston, 1742), 36. These lines rephrase Luke 1:46–7 and John 15:26. Mason's popular volume of poems was originally published in 1693, and it was reprinted continually throughout the eighteenth century. The first edition has the extended title *Begun by the Author of the Songs of Praise, and carried on by another Hand*. This edition and subsequent editions contains six of Mason's poems, with the remaining works attributed to Thomas Shepherd.

46. Rodger Payne observes that "Sarah's narrative in the hands of her husband was transformed into an anonymous account that mythologized and idealized its subject" (25), and Julie Ellison identifies one element of her account that her husband omits from his more theoretical version, that is, the social orientation of Sarah Edwards's piety (481).

47. Because he is identified only as "Mr. Williams of Hadley" and because there were several with this name in Hadley, there is no consensus about the identity of this man. Murray, 196, finds him to be William Williams, but Marsden, 243 and 359, identifies him as the Reverend Chester Williams and further describes him as "Sarah's sometimes nemesis." Chester Williams, minister of the First Church of Hadley, Massachusetts, was Jonathan Edwards's cousin and longstanding opponent, primarily regarding Williams's adherence to Arminianism. In his capacity as a member of the Hampshire Association of Churches, Williams sat on the 1750 council and voted for Jonathan Edwards's dismissal from the Northampton congregation (Marsden, 243, 245, and 359, and Winslow, 254). Jonathan Edwards writes that Williams "especially engaged against me" (*Works*, 16:323).

48. Samuel Buell, a young minister, was sent by the Fairfield Association of Clergy to study under Edwards before ordination and, according to Winslow, was "in charge" during Jonathan Edwards's absence in 1742. He had worked on an early revival initiative with Eleazar Wheelock and thus had prior experience in pulpit oratory (Dodds, 98–99, Marsden, 244–45, Miller, 204, and Winslow, 196, 204).

49. Amanda Porterfield first suggested Sarah Edwards's "artful" posture in her spiritual narrative. See *Feminine Spirituality in America from Sarah Edwards to Martha Graham* (Philadelphia: Temple UP, 1980), 22, 41, 47–48. Drawing on the work of Porterfield, Julie Ellison understands Sarah Edwards's dramatic spiritual revival as a carefully constructed demonstration to her husband's congregation of her saintliness and, by extension, her husband's pastoral efficacy (479–95).

50. Ralph Erskine, *Gospel Sonnets; or, Spiritual Songs in Six Parts* (Philadelphia, 1740), 256.

51. Ibid., 255–57.

52. In this final moment of introspection and self-revelation coupled with religious enthusiasm, Edwards makes a notable and exceptional claim of her humility before her community that exhibits the clear hierarchy of her eighteenth-century

society: "It was sweet to me, to see others before me in their divine attainments, and to follow after them to heaven. I thought I should rejoice to follow the Negro servants in the town to heaven" (16).

53. Gustafson, "Jonathan Edwards and the Reconstruction of 'Feminine' Speech," 205. See also Sandra M. Gustafson, *Eloquence Is Power: Oratory and Performance in Early America* (Chapel Hill and London: U North Carolina P, 2000), 69–71.

54. I am grateful to Steven Mintz for proposing the phrase "enlightened evangelism," which characterizes many of the themes and rhetorical features of Gill's narrative.

55. Anne Bradstreet, *The Works of Anne Bradstreet*, ed. Jeannine Hensley (Cambridge and London: Cambridge UP, 1967), 243.

56. *Works*, 16:792.

57. See especially 52, 55, and Burr, 262–63.

58. John Owen, *Phronema to pneumatos; or, The grace and duty of being spiritually-minded* (London, 1681).

59. See 96n43.

60. Payne, 34.

61. Ibid., 46.

62. Susan Juster's study of post-revolutionary women's conversion narratives finds that "the image of God . . . is most often that of a family member or personal friend," while male narratives cast the deity in hierarchical or contractual terms. See "'In a Different Voice': Male and Female Conversion in Post-Revolutionary America," *American Quarterly* 41.1 (1989): 40–43. However, in the earlier eighteenth-century women's spiritual autobiographies, the authors draw on both modes of understanding their relationship with God.

63. See Roxeanne Harde's analysis of female authority, conversation, and authorship in Esther Edwards Burr's letter-journal, "I don't like strangers on the Sabbath': Theology and Subjectivity in the Journal of Esther Edwards Burr," *Legacy* 19.1 (2003): 18–25.

The Spiritual Narrative of Sarah Pierpont Edwards

1. See 97n47.

2. Rev. Peter Reynolds, pastor of the Enfield congregation, would later vote in support of Jonathan Edwards, in opposition to Edwards's dismissal from the First Church of Northampton (Marsden, 243–44, Winslow, 254).

3. Erskine, 256 ("The Valour and Victories of Faith").

4. The second quotation is from Rom. 8:35.

5. The scriptural quotation is from Rom. 8:33.

6. Edwards alludes to Rev. 5:5.

7. A phrasing common to seventeenth and eighteenth-century Calvinists, this is an allusion to Ps. 73:26, "My flesh and my heart faileth; but God is the strength of my heart, and portion for ever." See also Lam. 3:24, Ps. 16:5, Ps. 119:57, and Ps. 142:5.

8. Edwards alludes here to 1 Pet. 2:9, in which Christians are termed "a chosen generation, a royal priesthood, an holy nation."

9. See 97n48.

10. Sarah Edwards invokes the language of Matt. 21:16, this being a reference to Ps. 8:2.

11. Samuel Phelps and his wife, Miriam Austen Phelps, were neighbors of the Edwards family and members of the Northampton congregation (*Works*, 16:821).

12. Rev. Samuel Hopkins and Samuel Buell were members of the Yale class of 1741; Edwards delivered the graduation sermon (*Works*, 22:42). See also 94n8. Col. Timothy Dwight was a Northampton lawyer and Hampshire County judge. He and his wife Eleanor were the Edwards's next-door neighbors and close friends; they were also members of the congregation and figured among Jonathan Edwards's staunchest advocates. Their son Timothy married the Edwards's daughter Mary (Dodds, 100–101; Marsden, 358–59). Mr. and Mrs. Joseph Allen are listed on the seating chart for the 1737 Northampton meetinghouse (Marsden, 188). After studies at Yale, Job Strong of Northampton served as missionary to the Six Nations Indians in New York and New England. In 1749 he assumed the pulpit in Portsmouth, New Hampshire (Marsden, 339, 356, and Murray, 198).

13. Hymn 3:42 in Isaac Watts, *Hymns and Spiritual Songs in Three Books* (Boston, 1742), 316. See 96n44.

14. Sereno Edwards Dwight's publication places this on "Thursday, June 28th," but this is clearly an error because the events described in Edwards's journal take place between January 19 and February 4.

15. At this place in the text, Sereno Edwards Dwight adds a footnote to identify the verse by Isaac Watts as the "91st Hymn of the 2d Book." See Hymn 2:91 in Watts, *Hymns*, 212. Dwight adds that the themes of this hymn "concern the loveliness of Christ, the enjoyments and employments of heaven, and the christian's earnest desire of heavenly things."

16. In eighteenth-century optics, a "pencil" is a set of rays converging or diverging from a single point.

17. Edwards rephrases 2 Sam. 7:22.

18. Benjamin Sheldon, a militia captain in the French and Indian War, was a Northampton resident (*Works*, 16: 825). Sheldon and Edwards employ the language of Mal. 4:2.

19. Song 24, in Mason, 36. See also 97n45.

20. Mrs. P— is most likely Mrs. Seth Pomeroy, a church member and friend of the Edwards family.

21. Edwards refers to John 13–17.

22. *Penitential Cries* is Edwards's abbreviated title for John Mason's *Spiritual Songs; or, Songs of Praise with Penitential Cries to Almighty God.*

23. Deacon Moses Lyman, a member of the Northampton congregation and supporter of Jonathan Edwards, was the parishioner who initially approached the minister about the problem of children who were surreptitiously reading a midwives' handbook. This incident was one of a series of events that led to the minister's dismissal. Lyman moved to Goshen, Connecticut, in 1739 and corresponded with Jonathan Edwards after his move (*Works*, 16:96–98, 250–54; Dodds, 103; Marsden, 228; and Miller, 215).

24. Rev. Peter Clark, Jonathan Edwards's ministerial colleague and strong supporter from Salem Village, was called upon in 1750 to respond to Edwards's *Humble*

Inquiry, a controversial position paper largely concerning the halfway covenant (*Works*, 16:341–47; Winslow, 253).

25. Seth Pomeroy was a blacksmith and member of the Northampton congregation. A charismatic and often combative figure, he enjoyed the friendship of Jonathan and Sarah Edwards. Pomeroy would become a major in the provincial army in the 1770s (Marsden, 179 and 311; Winslow, 251).

26. Elizabeth Singer Rowe, *Devout Exercises of the Heart in Meditation and Soliloquy, Prayer, and Praise By the late Pious and Ingenious Mrs. Rowe*, ed. I. Watts (Boston, 1742), 37. See 96n44.

The Spiritual Narrative of Sarah Prince Gill

1. White's tract, *New England's Lamentations*.
2. Gill alludes to the barren fig tree in the parable of Luke 13:7.
3. Celebrated evangelist George Whitefield preached in Boston in 1739 and again in 1740. See also 94n10.
4. Gilbert Tennent, a Scotch-Irish Presbyterian, ranks with Jonathan Edwards and George Whitefield among evangelist leaders. A minister in Brunswick, New Jersey, and then Philadelphia, Tennent preached in Boston in December 1740. See Marsden, 215–16, and Allen Johnson, *Dictionary of American Biography*. 10 vols. (New York: Scribners, 1946), 17:366–68.
5. Samuel Cooper, pastor of the Brattle Square Church in Boston, was a recent Harvard graduate when Gill heard him preach (Johnson, 2:410–11).
6. Eleazar Wheelock, a founder of Dartmouth College, was one of a number of ministers who followed George Whitefield's example by traveling throughout New England in 1741 and 1742 as itinerant preachers. He eventually settled as minister in Lebanon Crank, Pennsylvania (*Works*, 16:85–86, and Marsden, 216–18).
7. The reference appears to be to Song of Sol. 11; however, the Song of Solomon has only eight chapters. The language and themes of Gill's comments on the sermon mirror those of Song of Sol. 3.
8. The passage that begins "Longings for the Salvation of Others" and ends with the words "discourse about any other object a burden" is found on the otherwise blank verso page. A cross mark directs the reader to this passage.
9. The ordinances of infant baptism and the Eucharist, which are considered the seals of the Covenant with God, were the only sacraments recognized by Gill's church.
10. This sentence is found on an otherwise blank verso page. The reader is directed to this passage by a cross marked in the journal.
11. To "walk" is a metaphorical expression for observing a code of daily conduct. See number 17 of the *Thirty-Nine Articles of Faith*: "They [the Elect] walk religiously in good works," in John H. Leith, ed., *Creeds of the Churches: A Reader in Christian Doctrine from the Bible to the Present* (Chicago: Aldine P, 1963), 269.
12. Rev. Jonathan Edwards served as a guest preacher at Old South Church on that and many other Sundays.
13. Gill's language echoes that of John 12:32.

14. This is a common misstatement of Matt. 12:33, "for the tree is known by his fruit." See also Luke 6:44.
15. Gill employs the metaphors of Rom. 8:15.
16. See Job 29:2.
17. This is most likely Rev. Gilbert Tennent.
18. The reference is to 1 Cor. 2. As Gill explains later in the entry, the "first closure with Christ" is the moment of conversion.
19. Rev. John Owen of Groton, Connecticut, was educated at Harvard College and served as minister of Groton from 1727 until his death in 1753 (*Works*, 16:54, and *New England historical and genealogical register* (Boston: New-England Historic Genealogical Society, 1864–), 11:70.
20. Gill alludes to Ps. 42:1, "As the hart panteth after the water brooks so panteth my soul after thee, O God," and replaces "hart" by "heart." She uses this expression frequently throughout her narrative, sometimes writing "hart."
21. The serpent in Gen. 3:1 is described as "subtil."
22. Gill uses the language of Isa. 9:6.
23. Gill refers to Dan. 6 and 2 Tim. 4:17.
24. Isaac Watts, Hymn 115 in *Hymns*, 91.
25. Gill alludes to Matt. 13:45–46.
26. In eighteenth- and nineteenth-century religious discourse, "frames" is a term for emotional states used to discern the reality of spiritual life.
27. Deborah Prince, Gill's eldest sister, died on July 20, 1744.
28. Gill refers here to her only brother, Thomas, and to Mercy, who at this time was the oldest daughter in the Prince family.
29. Gill's metaphor of the light of God's countenance is found in Ps. 4:6, 44:3, 89:15, and 90:8.
30. See Thomas Prince, *The sovereign God acknowledged and blessed, both in giving and taking away: A sermon occasioned by the decease of Mrs. Deborah Prince, on Friday July 20. 1744* (Boston, 1744).
31. Joseph Sewall was the senior minister at Boston's Old South Church where Thomas Prince, Sarah Prince Gill's father, was ordained and served as minister.
32. This entry largely paraphrases Isa. 57:15.
33. Gill alludes to Eph. 3:19.
34. Gill alludes to Hos. 10:12.
35. Hymn 2:20 in Watts, *Hymns*, 142. These lines are also found in Rowe, 34. Elizabeth Singer Rowe's popular book provided the model for Gill's personal meditation, such that Gill's journal entry of December 25, 1762, duplicates Rowe's Exercise No. 8. See also 96n44.
36. The "other papers" are not extant.
37. Exercise 31 appears on page 120 of the 1742 edition of Rowe's *Devout Exercises*.
38. This phrase is from Eph. 3:8.
39. The manuscript of Gill's devout exercises is not extant. However, ten of her exercises were published in 1771 as an appendix to her funeral sermon preached by John Hunt and reprinted again in 1799. See John Hunt, *A Sermon Occasioned by the Death of Mrs. Sarah Gill, Late Consort to Mr. Moses Gill, Merchant, and Preached at the South-Church in Boston the Lords's-Day after her Decease* (Boston, 1771).

40. Gill drew lines through the adjective "hard" in an attempt to delete the word. This is one of her two editorial amendments of note in the manuscript.

41. See 99n16.

42. Psalm 27, Part 1, in Isaac Watts, *The Psalms of David, Imitated in the Language of the New Testament, and Apply'd to the Christian State and Worship* (Boston, 1741), 58.

43. Gill refers here to an offer of marriage. See Burr, 232–33.

44. Regarding the date in the body of the journal entry, Gill originally wrote "Oct.," then drew a single line through the word and wrote "Nov." above it. There is an error in the date of the journal entry, or the date in the journal entry, or both.

45. Gill invokes Christ's final words in Mark 14:36. See also Matt. 26:42.

46. See Matt. 22: 36–40.

47. In a marginal note Gill writes, "From Psalm 11.2." This passage is not a scriptural quotation, but a lyric meditation on the themes of Psalms 11 and 12 found in ll.25–36 of Isaac Watts's hymn "The Comparison and Complaint" in Watts, *Horæ Lyricæ. Poems Chiefly of the Lyric Kind, in Three Books* (New York, 1750), 56.

48. The Sermon on the Mount is found in Matt. 5–7 and contains many of Christ's parables, the Lord's Prayer, the Beatitudes, and commentary on the law.

49. 1 John does not have eight chapters. Gill most likely meant 1 John 1:1–4.

50. During the French and Indian War, John Campbell, Earl of Loudoun, led English forces against the French in Canada. In the seventeenth century the Church Militant stood guard to protect churchgoers on the Sabbath from Indians and wolves. The Church Militant of the eighteenth century is also identified as an organization whose main activity was teaching boys to march and to shoot. See Alice Morse Earle, *The Sabbath in Puritan New England* (1891; reprint, Williamstown, MA: Corner House, 1969), 19, and Justin Winsor, ed., *The Memorial History of Boston, Including Suffolk County, Massachusetts*, 4 vols. (Boston: James R. Osgood, 1881), 2:481. Gill's metaphorical use of this term is broader than the above, and suggests the entire community of believers.

51. Mrs. Rowe uses the term "Darling sin" in *Devout Exercises* to suggest a vice that is especially difficult to forego.

52. Hymn II:139 in Watts, *Hymns*, 253.

53. "Pharoah's chariots" refers to the Egyptian troops sent after the Hebrews who were escaping Egyptian bondage as told in Ex. 13–14. Ex. 14:25 notes that the Egyptian troops removed the wheels and "drave them heavily" yet perished in their pursuit.

54. Gill alludes to Heb. 4:16.

55. Frederick II ruled Prussia from 1740 to 1786. Although his primary objective was political and military power, he adhered to his father's commitment to the Protestant faith.

56. David Brainerd was a missionary to the Delaware Indians in a settlement near Trenton, New Jersey. Parts of his diary were published in America in 1746, and other portions were included in Jonathan Edwards's 1749 publication, *The Life of David Brainerd*. This book had great popular success, with 1,953 subscriptions for the first edition. Gill would have "received refreshment" from reading Brainerd's diary because Brainerd's struggle to perceive the sovereignty of God parallels Gill's. See *Works*, 16:250, and Marsden, 329–33.

57. Gill uses the language of Ps. 6:6.
58. Gill refers to the Song of Solomon as sol song, which is the abbreviation used in Isaac Watts's *Hymns*.
59. These passages are from Song of Sol. 4:7–8.
60. This couplet is found in Rowe, 54.
61. In the letter dated May 24, 1757, Esther Edwards Burr writes that Mrs. Oliver condemned Mrs. Holland's malicious gossip regarding Gill (Burr, 262–63).
62. Gill paraphrases Mark 14:36.
63. S—— and C—— are unidentified friends and perhaps members of the Old South Church women's prayer group to which Gill belonged.
64. Gill invokes the language of Jer. 9:15 and 23:15, and Lam. 3:19.
65. This is an allusion to 2 Kings 5:1–14.
66. Gill refers to Owen's *Phronema to pneumatos* and Samuel Boyse's translation of François de Salignac de La Mothe Fénélon, *A demonstration of the existence of God: deduced from the knowledge of nature, and more particularly from that of man* (London, 1749).
67. Thomas Prince's important library belongs to the New Old South Church in Boston, but it is currently housed in the Boston Public Library. The collection consists of manuscripts and books on the history of New England, theological works that were published in America and Europe, and general books that were published in New England. The Prince Library's catalog lists more than two thousand items, not the least of which are two of the five known copies of the *Bay Psalm Book*. See *The Prince Library: A Catalogue of the Collection of Books and Manuscripts Which Formerly Belonged to the Reverend Thomas Prince and Was by Him Bequeathed to the Old South Church and Is Now Deposited in the Public Library of the City of Boston* (Boston: Alfred Mudge and Sons, 1870).
68. In her letter of May 24, 1757, Esther Edwards Burr refers to a relationship between Sarah Prince and "Doctor Somebody," who is also called "Doctor Fickle" in other letters. Karlsen and Crumpacker have identified "the doctor" as Alexander Cumming. After unsuccessfully courting Sarah Prince, Cumming married Eunice Polk. Eunice remained jealous of her husband's former courtship of Gill. Ironically Alexander Cumming became the associate pastor of the Old South Church after Thomas Prince's death (Burr, 263n46).
69. The scriptural use of the word "lees" connotes the perilous comfort of worldly fortunes. See Jer. 48:11, Isa. 25:6, and Zeph. 1:12.
70. This is probably Mrs. Holland. See 50 and 103n61.
71. The opening reference to "the King" is most likely, for this British citizen, the king of England.
72. Gill alludes to James 3:11. See also Exod. 15:23, Num. 5, and Rev. 8:11.
73. See Ps. 120:5.
74. Gill quotes most likely from Dr. John Guyse, an English reformed minister and popular author who, with Dr. Isaac Watts, published the London edition of Jonathan Edwards's *A Faithful Narrative* in 1737.
75. Aminadab is identified in Exod. 6:23, Ruth 4:19–20, and Matt. 1:4.
76. Gill uses the metaphors of Job 25:6
77. Massachusetts experienced a sizeable earthquake on the morning of Tuesday, November 18, 1755, which Esther Edwards Burr documents in her letter of the

same day (167). That Burr felt the tremors in New Jersey is indicative of its strength and the fear it produced. Thomas Prince and other ministers used the earthquake as the subject of cautionary sermons.

78. Gill alludes to Ps. 55:6.

79. The public distress is probably the French and Indian War of 1754–1761, one of the few references to this war in the journal.

80. Gill alludes to Jer. 2:13.

81. See xxiii.

82. The metaphor of God's punishing rod is common throughout the scriptures. See especially Prov. 10:13 and 13:24.

83. Gill's statement that "we had intended to Live together" likely means that Gill was repeatedly invited by Esther Edwards Burr and Aaron Burr to be their guest in Newark. It was common throughout the eighteenth century for unmarried women to make extended visits to the home of married female friends. Esther Burr extends insistent invitations throughout her correspondence with Gill. For example, on January 27, 1755, Burr writes about her tentative plans to travel to Boston, and adds, "But this depend on without ifs and ands that if I do go I'll not return without you with me—I am resolved on't" (Burr, 85). Then, on February 7, 1755, she writes, "My dear, I depend on your coming here before or by next fall. . . . [Mr Burr] gives me a great charge to tell you that he depends on your coming. . . . We are afraid you don't think of it in ernest" (Burr, 89). Although she never made the promised trip, Gill clearly thought of it "in ernest."

84. The relict, or widow, is, of course, Gill's friend and correspondent Esther Edwards Burr.

85. Gill alludes to Exod. 12:8 and Num. 9:11.

86. Gill uses the image of Matt. 14:35–36.

87. Gill rephrases "the valley of the shadow of death" in Ps. 23:4.

88. This metaphor is found in Song of Sol. 4:16.

89. Gill refers to either the death of her sister Deborah in 1744 or that of Mercy in 1752.

90. Where Gill uses the word "Painfull," one should understand "painstaking."

91. Thomas Prince's ministerial colleague at Old South Church was Joseph Sewall.

92. The "Marriage Intentions of Sarah Prince and Moses Gill" was published on March 1, 1759. See A Volume of records relating to the early history of Boston, containing Boston marriages from 1752 to 1809 (Boston: Municipal Printing Office, 1903).

93. When Gill asserts that in marriage she has been made "head of a family," she indicates her position as domestic head of the household and spiritual leader of the servants in the Gill home. See the following entry as evidence of her devotion to this role.

94. Massachusetts Bay School Law, which was passed in 1642 and was still in effect during Gill's lifetime, required that masters of households had to instruct their servants and their children in the catechism at least once a week. See Mortimer Jerome Adler, ed., The Annals of America: Great Issues in American Life: A Conspectus, 4 vols. (Chicago: Encyclopaedia Britannica, 1968), 1:170–71.

95. During the search for a new pastor after Thomas Prince's death in 1758, many pastors were invited for short trial periods, but the church was unable to decide

on a permanent appointment. Finally, in 1760, Alexander Cumming was invited to become the associate pastor, but his tenure was controversial from the beginning. The *Boston Gazette* published a vicious letter from an "anonymous countryman" who criticized Cumming and the Old South Church for the sumptuousness of his ordination banquet. Rebuttals followed, and the matter was kept alive for several weeks in the newspaper. Furthermore, several church members protested Cumming's sermons as excessively metaphysical. Just as the congregation began to accept Cumming, he died suddenly in 1763. Dissension existed regarding other issues also. As recorded in the church records by Dr. Sewall, there were protracted squabbles over pew allocation and ownership. In addition, the Old South Church was embroiled in a decade-long debate over the selection of a psalter, with the *Bay Psalm Book*, Watts's hymnody, and Tate and Brady's psalm book being among the choices. See Hamilton Andrews Hill, *History of the Old South Church*. 2 vols. (Cambridge: Riverside P, 1890), 2:32–8, 61–64, and 71.

96. This is a rephrasing of Matt. 18:20.

97. Ichabod means "the glory is departed from Israel." See 1 Sam. 4:19–22.

98. Gill uses the language of Deut. 16:3.

99. Gill rephrases Jer. 2:17. See also Jer. 4:18.

100. Nathaniel Potter resigned from his post at the Church of Christ at Brookline, Massachusetts, after a salary dispute with church elders. After Thomas Prince's death, Potter was invited to preach at the Old South Church for six consecutive Sundays. The congregation enjoyed his sermons, but the scandal surrounding his resignation precluded an offer of a permanent post at the Old South Church (Hill, 2: 48–9).

101. Gill quotes from her father's poetic interpretation of Ps. 51. See Thomas Prince, "Psalm LI" in *The Psalms, Hymns, & Spiritual Songs, of the Old and New Testament, Failthfully translated into English Metre* (Boston, 1758), 91.

102. Gill quotes Ps. 51:11.

103. See Prov. 26:11 and 2 Pet. 2:22, as well as Jonathan Edwards's use of this scriptural passage in "Personal Narrative" in *Works*, 16:791.

104. X is Gill's symbol for Christ.

105. 1 Sam. 7:12 states that "Samuel took a stone . . . and called the name of it Ebenezer, saying, Hitherto hath the Lord helped us."

106. Gill identifies the minister in a marginal note as "a Mr Coops," which is most likely a reference to Mr. Cooper.

107. Gill uses the language of Gen. 1:2.

108. These metaphors are found in Hos. 11:4.

109. Gill edited this sentence in her journal. She originally wrote, "never more be my own or the Words, or Lusts, but Love, Fear, serve, and delight in thee Forever" but drew a line through the words "or Lusts."

110. The initial use of this common scriptural metaphor is Exod. 34:15.

111. See 103n68.

112. Watts, Hymn 123 in *Hymns*, 97.

113. Consistent with her use of the symbol X for Christ, Gill identifies the antichrist as "anti X."

114. Xn is Gill's shorthand for Christian.

115. Gill misquotes Ps. 81:10.
116. Gill refers to Jer. 20:2–4, in which God renames Pashur, who had imprisoned Jeremiah the prophet, as Magormissabib because God knows him as "a terror to thyself, and to all thy friends."

Works Cited

Adler, Mortimer Jerome. Ed. *The Annals of America: Great Issues in American Life: A Conspectus.* 4 vols. Chicago: Encyclopaedia Britannica, 1968.

Ames, William. *The Marrow of Conversion.* 1629. Ed. and trans. John D. Eusden. Grand Rapids, MI: Baker Books, 1968.

Bradstreet, Anne. *The Works of Anne Bradstreet.* Ed. Jeannine Hensley. Cambridge and London: Cambridge UP, 1967.

Burr, Esther Edwards. *The Journal of Esther Edwards Burr, 1754–1757.* Ed. Carol F. Karlsen and Laurie Crumpacker. New Haven and London: Yale UP, 1984.

Butler, Jon. "Enthusiasm Described and Decried: The Great Awakening as Interpretive Fiction." *Journal of American History* 69.2 (1982): 305–25.

Caldwell, Patricia. *The Puritan Conversion Narrative: The Beginnings of American Expression.* Cambridge: Cambridge UP, 1983.

Conforti, Joseph. "The Invention of the Great Awakening, 1795–1842." *Early American Literature* 26.2 (1991): 99–118.

———. *Jonathan Edwards, Religious Tradition, and American Culture.* Chapel Hill and London: U North Carolina P, 1995.

Cotton, John. *The Way of the Churches of Christ in New-England.* London, 1645.

Dodds, Elisabeth D. *Marriage to a Difficult Man: The "Uncommon Union" of Jonathan and Sarah Edwards.* Philadelphia: Westminster P, 1972.

Dwight, Sereno Edwards. *The Life of President Edwards.* Vol. 1 of *The Works of President Edwards, with a Memoir of His Life.* Ed. Sereno Edwards Dwight. 10 vols. New York, 1830.

Earle, Alice Morse. *The Sabbath in Puritan New England.* 1891. Reprint, Williamstown, MA: Corner House, 1969.

Edwards, Jonathan. *The Works of Jonathan Edwards.* 22 vols. to date. Ed. Perry Miller, John E. Smith, and Harry S. Stout. New Haven: Yale UP, 1957– .

Edwards, Sarah Pierpont. "On Tuesday night, Jan. 19, 1742." In *The Life of President Edwards.* Vol. 1 of *The Works of President Edwards, with a Memoir of His Life.* Ed. Sereno Edwards Dwight. 10 vols. New York, 1830. 171–86.

Ellison, Julie. "The Sociology of 'Holy Indifference': Sarah Edwards' Narrative." *American Literature* 56 (December 1984): 479–95.

Erskine, Ralph. *Gospel Sonnets; or, Spiritual Songs in Six Parts.* Philadelphia, 1740.

Fénélon, François de Salignac de La Mothe, *A demonstration of the existence of God: deduced from the knowledge of nature, and more particularly from that of man*. Trans. Samuel Boyse. London, 1749.

Gustafson, Sandra M. "Jonathan Edwards and the Reconstruction of 'Feminine' Speech." *American Literary History* 6 (Summer 1994): 185–212.

———. *Eloquence Is Power: Oratory and Performance in Early America*. Chapel Hill and London: U North Carolina P, 2000.

Hambrick-Stowe, Charles E. *The Practice of Piety: Puritan Devotional Disciplines in Seventeenth Century New England*. Chapel Hill and London: U North Carolina P, 1986.

Harde, Roxanne. "'I don't like strangers on the Sabbath': Theology and Subjectivity in the Journal of Esther Edwards Burr." *Legacy* 19.1 (2003): 18–25.

Hill, Hamilton Andrews. *History of the Old South Church*. 2 vols. Cambridge: Riverside P, 1890.

Hopkins, Samuel. Appendix 2, "Containing a Short Sketch of Mrs. Edwards's Life and Character," in *The Life and Character of the Late Reverend Mr. Jonathan Edwards*. Boston, 1852, 92–98.

Hunt, John. *A Sermon Occasioned by the Death of Mrs. Sarah Gill, Late Consort to Mr. Moses Gill, Merchant, and Preached at the South-Church in Boston the Lord's-Day after her Decease*. Boston, 1771.

Johnson, Allen. *Dictionary of American Biography*. 10 vols. New York: Scribners, 1946.

Juster, Susan. "'In a Different Voice': Male and Female Conversion in Post-Revolutionary America." *American Quarterly* 41.1 (1989): 39–62.

Leith, John H. Ed. *Creeds of the Churches: A Reader in Christian Doctrine from the Bible to the Present*. Chicago: Aldine P, 1963.

Marsden, George M. *Jonathan Edwards: A Life*. New Haven and London: Yale UP, 2003.

Mason, John. *Spiritual Songs; or, Songs of Praise with Penitential Cries to Almighty God*. Boston, 1742.

McCulley, Sue Lane Brady. *From the Rhetoric of Ramus to the Rhetoric of the Revolution*. Ph.D. diss., University of Houston, 2002.

Miller, Perry. *Jonathan Edwards*. New York: William Sloan, 1949.

Morgan, Edmund S. *Visible Saints: The History of a Puritan Idea*. Ithaca and London: Cornell UP, 1963.

Murray, Iain H. *Jonathan Edwards: A New Biography*. Carlisle, PA: Banner of Truth Trust, 1988.

The New England historical and genealogical register. Boston: New-England Historic Genealogical Society, 1864– .

Owen, John. *Phronema to pneumatos; or, The grace and duty of being spiritually-minded*. London, 1681.

Works Cited

Payne, Rodger M. *The Self and the Sacred: Conversion and Autobiography in Early American Protestantism.* Knoxville: U of Tennessee P, 1998.

Porterfield, Amanda. *Feminine Spirituality in America from Sarah Edwards to Martha Graham.* Philadelphia: Temple UP, 1980.

Prince, Thomas. *The Psalms, Hymns, & Spiritual Songs, of the Old and New Testament, Failthfully translated into English Metre.* Boston, 1758.

————. *The sovereign God acknowledged and blessed, both in giving and taking away: A sermon occasioned by the decease of Mrs. Deborah Prince, on Friday July 20. 1744.* Boston, 1744.

The Prince Library: A Catalogue of the Collection of Books and Manuscripts Which Formerly Belonged to the Reverend Thomas Prince and Was by Him Bequeathed to the Old South Church and Is Now Deposited in the Public Library of the City of Boston. Boston, Alfred Mudge and Sons, 1870.

Rowe, Elizabeth Singer. *Devout Exercises of the Heart: In meditation and soliloquy, prayer and praise, by the late pious and ingenious Mrs. Rowe; Review'd and published at her request, by I. Watts, D.D.* Boston, 1742.

Shea, Daniel B. *Spiritual Autobiography in Early America.* Princeton: Princeton UP, 1968.

Shea, William M. "Jonathan Edwards and Sarah Pierpont." In *Foundations of Religious Literacy.* Ed. John V. Apczynski. Chico, CA: Scholars P, 1983. 107–26.

Shepard, Thomas. *The Parable of the Ten Virgins.* Vol. 2. London, 1660.

Tracy, Joseph. *The Great Awakening: A History of the Revival of Religion in the Time of Edwards and Whitefield.* Boston, 1842.

Tracy, Patricia. *Jonathan Edwards, Pastor: Religion and Society in Eighteenth-Century Northampton.* New York: Hill and Wang, 1980.

A Volume of relating to the early history of Boston, containing Boston marriages from 1752 to 1809. Boston: Municipal Printing Office, 1903.

Walker, Williston. *The Creeds and Platforms of Congregationalism.* Philadelphia: Pilgrim P, 1960.

Watts, Isaac. *Horæ Lyricæ. Poems Chiefly of the Lyric Kind, in Three Books.* New York, 1750.

————. *Hymns and Spiritual Songs in Three Books.* Boston, 1742.

————. *The Psalms of David, Imitated in the Language of the New Testament, and Apply'd to the Christian State and Worship.* Boston, 1741.

White, John. *New England's Lamentations: Under Three Heads, the Decay of the Power of Godliness; The Danger of Arminian Principles; The Declining State of our Church Order, Government, and Discipline.* Boston, 1734.

Whitefield, George. *George Whitefield's Journals.* Edinburgh: Banner of Truth Trust, 1960.

Winslow, Ola Elizabeth. *Jonathan Edwards, 1703–1758.* New York: Macmillan, 1940.

Works Cited

Winsor, Justin, ed. *The Memorial History of Boston, Including Suffolk County, Massachusetts.* 4 vols. Boston, James R. Osgood, 1881.

Yarbrough, Stephen R., and John C. Adams. *Delightful Conviction: Jonathan Edwards and the Rhetoric of Conversion.* Westport, CT, and London: Greenwood P, 1993.

Index

The abbreviation SPE refers to Sarah Pierpont Edwards, SPG to Sarah Prince Gill, JE to Jonathan Edwards, and MG to Moses Gill.

Adams, John C., 93n4
Allen, Joseph, 99n12; in SPE's spiritual narrative, 6
Ames, William, xv, xxv

Boyse, Samuel: in SPG's spiritual narrative, 58
Bradstreet, Anne, xxxvii
Brainerd, David, 102n56; JE's biography of, xv; in SPG's spiritual narrative, 47
Buell, Samuel, xxxii, 97n48, 99n12; in SPE's spiritual narrative, 4–8, 11, 14, 15
Burr, Aaron, xx, xxvi; correspondence with SPG, xxiii, 104n83; death of, xx, xxiii; and JE, xxvi; in SPG's spiritual narrative, 67–68, 69, 104n83; on women and marriage, xxiii
Burr, Aaron, Jr. (grandson of SPE and JE), xxi
Burr, Esther Edwards (daughter of SPE and JE), xx, xxiv; correspondence with SPE, xx, xxi; death of, xxi, xxiii, 72; on Elizabeth Singer Rowe and Isaac Watts, 97n44; and SPG, xxii–xxiii; in SPG's spiritual narrative, 67–68, 71–72
Burr, Sally (granddaughter of SPE and JE), xxi
Butler, Jon, 94n11

Caldwell, Patricia, xiii, 95n30, 96n34, 96n42
Clark, Peter, 99n24; in SPE's spiritual narrative, 15

College of New Jersey (later Princeton University), xvi, xx, xxi
Conforti, Joseph, 94n11
conversion, xxv–xxvi; renewed, xxv–xxvi. See also narratives, conversion
covenant, half-way, 95n16; JE's position on, xix, 99n24
Cooper, Samuel, 100n5; in SPG's spiritual narrative, 18–19, 23, 105n106
Cotton, John, xxvi, 96n34
Cumming, Alexander, 103n68, 104n95; in SPG's spiritual narrative, 86

Dodds, Elisabeth D., 93n3, 95n24, 97n48, 99n12
Dwight, Eleanor, 99n12; in SPE's spiritual narrative, 6
Dwight, Mary Edwards (daughter of SPE and JE), xx
Dwight, Sereno Edwards (grandson of SPE and JE), 95n14; and The Life of President Edwards, ix, xix
Dwight, Col. Timothy, 99n12
Dwight, Timothy (son-in-law of SPE and JE), xx

Edwards, Esther. See Burr, Esther Edwards
Edwards, Lucy (daughter of SPE and JE), xx
Edwards, Mary. See Dwight, Mary Edwards
Edwards, Jonathan
—on church membership, xv–xvi, xix, 95n16
—courtship and marriage of, xiv, xvi–xviii
—death of, xxi
—and George Whitefield, xvii
—and Isaac Watts, 96n44, 103n74
—"New Light" ministry of, xv–xvi

Edwards, Jonathan (cont.)
—Northampton ministry of, xvi–xx
—as president of the College of New
  Jersey, xvi, xxi
—reputation of, as theologian and orator,
  xiv–xv, xvii–xviii
—on sacraments, xv–xvi, xix
—Stockbridge ministry of, xx
—and Thomas Prince, xxi
—works: "The Curse of Meroz," 95n18;
  Divine and Supernatural Light, xiv; *A
  Faithful Narrative of the Surprising Work
  of God in the Conversion of Many Hundred
  Souls in Northampton*, xv, xvii, 96n37;
  Freedom of the Will, xiv; "Humble
  Inquiry," 95n16; "Images of Divine
  Things," xiv; *The Life of Brainerd*, xv,
  47; "Misrepresentations Corrected,"
  95n16; "Narrative of the Communion
  Controversy," 95n17; *The Nature of True
  Virtue*, xiv; *A Personal Narrative*, xiv, xxvi,
  xxxvii, 93n7, 105n103; "On Sarah
  Pierpont," xiv; "Self-Examination and
  the Lord's Supper," 95n17; "Sinners in
  the Hands of an Angry God," xv; *Some
  Thoughts Concerning the Present Revival of
  Religion*, xv, xviii, xxvi, 96n41; *Treatise
  on Religion Affections*, xiv, 93n5, 95n15
Edwards, Jonathan (son of JE and SPE), xvii
Edwards, Sarah. *See* Porter, Sarah Edwards
Edwards, Sarah Pierpont, **xxviii**
—conversion of, xviii, xxvii
—courtship and marriage of, xvi–xvii
—death of, xxi
—and Deborah Prince, xxi–xxii
—described by George Whitefield, xvii
—described by JE, xiv
—described by Samuel Hopkins, xvii
—dispute with Northampton congregation of, xx
—education and early life of, xiii–xiv, xvi
—as mother, xvii–xviii, xx–xxi
—as partner in JE's ministry, xvi,
  xvi–xviii, xx, xxxi–xxxv
—spiritual narrative of: authorial ethos of,
  xlii–xliii; JE's use of, xvii–xix, 93n7;

literary features of, xxviii–xxxi, xl–xli;
  physical manifestations of spirituality
  in, xviii, xxix–xxx, xxxiv, xliii; and
  popular literature, xxx–xxxiv;
  provenance and publication history
  of, ix, xiii, xviii–xix; reference to JE's
  ministry in, xxxi–xxxv, xlii–xliii;
  rhetorical situation, xiii–xiv, xviii,
  xxxi–xxxv; and scripture, xxx, xxxiv;
  social imperative of, xxxi,
  xxxiii–xxxiv
Ellison, Julie, 93n7, 97n49
enlightenment: relationship to evangelism,
  xxxix–xl
Erskine, Ralph: in SPE's spiritual narrative,
  xxxii–xxxiii, 2

Fénélon, François de Salignac de La
  Mothe, 103n66
Foster, Hannah Webster, xliii
Fuller, Margaret, xliv

Gill, Moses, xxiv, 104n92; in SPG's spiritual
  narrative, 75, 76
Gill, Sarah Prince, **xxxvi**
—and Aaron Burr Sr., xxiii, 67–68, 69
—conversion of, xxxv–xxxvi, 21
—death of, xxiv; family deaths, xxiii,
  xxiv, 25–27
—education and early life of, xxii–xxiii
—and Esther Edwards Burr, xxii–xxiii,
  67–68, 71–72
—and marriage, xxiii; to MG, xxiii–xxiv,
  75, 76
—publication of devout exercises,
  101n39
—spiritual narrative of: affections in,
  xl–xli; authorial ethos in, xlii–xliii;
  and church doctrine, xxxvi–xxxvii;
  enlightenment values reflected in,
  xxxv, xxxix–xli; JE's *The Life of Brainerd*
  in, 47; and linguistic inadequacy,
  xxxviii–xxxix; literary features of,
  xxxv, xxxix–xl; on public events,

xli–xliii; on the ministry of Old South Church, xli–xlii; and popular literature, xxxviii; provenance of, ix–x; rhetorical situation of, xiii–xiv, xxxv; and scripture, xxxvii–xxxviii; social imperative of, xli–xlii

Great Awakening, xvii–xviii, xxii, xxiv, xxxv; as a disputed term, 94n11

Gustafson, Sandra, xxxiv, 93n7, 98n53

Guyse, John, 103n74

Hambrick-Stowe, Charles E., xxv, 95n30

Harde, Roxanne, 98n63

Hooker, Thomas (great-grandfather of SPE), xvi

Hopkins, Samuel, xx, 94n8, 99n12; description of SPE, xvii; in SPE's spiritual narrative, 6

Hunt, John, 101n39

Juster, Susan, 98n62

Lyman, Moses, 99n23; in SPE's spiritual narrative, 14

Marsden, George M., 93n3

Mason, John, 97n45; in SPE's spiritual narrative, xxx, xxxiv, 10, 14, 97n45, 99n22

Miller, Perry, 93n3

Mintz, Steven, 98n54

Morgan, Edmund, xxv, 95n30

Murray, Iain H., 93n3

narratives, conversion, xiii, xxiv–xxv; female-authored, xiii, 96n36, 98n62; JE's directives on, xvi, xix, xxvi; literary features of, xxvii, xxxix; oral relation of, xxvi–xxvii; as requirement for church membership, xv, xvi, xix, xxvi; scholarship on, 95n30; seventeenth-century Puritan directives on, xxiv–xxvi; uses of, xxvi–xxvii. *See also* Edwards, Jonathan—Works: *A Personal Narrative*; narratives, spiritual

narratives, spiritual, xliii; and novels, xliii–xliv; relationship to conversion narrative, xxiv, xxvii–xxviii, xxxv–xxxvii. *See also* narratives, conversion

"New Light" theology, xv–xvi, xxvi

Owen, John, 101n19; in SPG's spiritual narrative, xxxviii, 21, 57–58, 103n66

Payne, Rodger M., xxvi–xxvii, xxx, xxxi, xxxv, xxxix–xl, 96n30, 96n38, 96n42, 97n46

Phelps, Samuel, 99n11; in SPE's spiritual narrative, 5, 15

Pierpont, James (father of SPE), xvi

Pierpont, Mary Hooker (mother of SPE), xvi

Pomeroy, Seth and Mrs., 99n20, 100n25; in SPE's spiritual narrative, 11, 15

Porter, Sarah Edwards (daughter of SPE and JE), xvii, xx

Porterfield, Amanda, 97n49

Potter, Nathaniel, 105n100; in SPG's spiritual narrative, 77

Prince, Deborah (mother of SPG), xxi–xxii; absence from SPG's spiritual narrative of, xxiii; and SPE, xxi–xxii

Prince, Deborah (sister of SPG), xxii; in SPG's spiritual narrative, 25–27

Prince, Grace (sister of SPG), xxii

Prince, Mercy (sister of SPG), xxii, xxiii; in SPG's spiritual narrative, 26, 67, 72

Prince, Thomas (brother of SPG), xxii; in SPG's spiritual narrative, 26, 67

Prince, Thomas (father of SPG) xxi–xxii; and JE, xxi, 95n24; library of, xxii, 103n67; ministry of, xxii; in SPG's spiritual narrative, 26, 28, 58, 68,

Prince, Thomas (cont.)
74–75, 87, 105n101; *The Psalms,
Hymns, & Spiritual Songs, of the Old and
New Testament*, 78, 105n101

Reynolds, Peter, 98n2; in SPE's spiritual
narrative, 1–2
Rowe, Elizabeth Singer, 96n44; in SPE's
spiritual narrative, xxx, 15; in SPG's
spiritual narrative, xxxviii, 31–32,
101n35, 101n37, 102n51, 103n60

Sewall, Joseph, xxii, 104n91; in SPG's
spiritual narrative, 28
Shea, Daniel B., 96n43
Shea, William M., 93n7
Sheldon, Benjamin, 99n18; in SPE's
spiritual narrative, 9
Shepard, Thomas, xxiv–xxvi
Stoddard, Solomon (grandfather of JE),
xv–xvi, xvii, xix
Stowe, Harriet Beecher, xliii–xliv
Strong, Job, 99n12; in SPE's spiritual
narrative, 6

Tennent, Gilbert, 100n4; in SPG's spiritual
narrative, 17, 20, 101n17

Tracy, Joseph, 94n11
Tracy, Patricia, 93n3

Watts, Isaac, xxx, 96n44, 104n95; and JE,
103n74; in SPE's spiritual narrative,
6, 7; in SPG's spiritual narrative, 23,
29, 102n42, 102n47, 102n52,
105n112
Wheelock, Eleazar, 97n48, 100n6; in
SPG's spiritual narrative, 18
White, John: in SPG's spiritual narrative,
xxii, xxxviii, 17
Whitefield, George, 94n10; description of
SPE, xvii; as guest of JE and SPE, xvii;
in SPG's spiritual narrative, xli, 17,
28, 29, 43, 91
Willet, Thomas (great-grandfather of
SPE), xvi
Williams, Chester, xxxi–xxxii; confused
with William Williams, 97n47; in
SPE's spiritual narrative 1, 9, 10
Williams, Israel, xix
Williams, William, 97n47
Winslow, Ola Elizabeth, 93n3

Yarbrough, Stephen R., 93n4

The Silent and Soft Communion was designed and typeset on a Macintosh computer system using QuarkXPress software. The body text is set in 11/13 Joanna and display type is set in Ovidius. This book was designed and typeset by Stephanie Thompson and manufactured by Thomson-Shore, Inc.